Jack Chi

by

May Conway

This book is a work of fiction. Names, characters, places, and incidents either are the product of the author's imagination or are used fictitiously. Any resemblance to actual persons, living or dead, events or locales, is entirely coincidental.

Copyright © 2023 May Conway
All Rights Reserved

To my boys, my daily inspiration.

One - The House

Chapter One

Tiny. Very small. Diminutive. A teeny, tiny, fur ball of a dog. Small, that was Jack Chi. A small blur of fur who ran around as fast as four small paws could carry him. He was, of course, a cross between a Jack Russell Terrier and a Chihuahua, but he wouldn't earn his name formally for three chaotic years.

Jack Chi stood (if you could get him to stand) nine old inches tall at the shoulder. That's about the thickness of six good books or perhaps two cushions. If he stood on his hind legs and stretched up really tall, he could just about reach up with his snuffly black nose to sniff things on the coffee table. He was white and fluffy all over, except for darker tan patches over his eyes and ears, with black tips to his ears and a big, black splodge at the base of his waggy tail. His dark eyes were large, slightly bulgy as all Chihuahuas' eyes are and he had dark lines around them just as if someone had drawn around those eyes with a black eyeliner pen. This made his eyes appear larger and prettier, but when he was scared he would show the white of his eyes, betraying his Chihuahua lineage even more. However, the long, fluffy fur on his face softened his big eyes and the overall effect was one very cute and attractive (if tiny) dog. His right ear was definitely Chi and, when he was excited or trying to pay attention, it stood up like a bat's ear, tall and quivering to listen, the other ear was all Jack and bent out to the side at a right angle, no matter the occasion.

But Jack had grown up with the wrong crowd. It wasn't his fault of course, but conditions were very overcrowded at the dog hoarder human's house and the other dogs were often nasty and pushed the tiny dog out of their way. He had had a happy enough puppyhood, even though he was the runt of the litter. His Chihuahua mum had been an efficient, if timid mother, and often couldn't protect him, so he quickly had to find his own way to deal with the bigger dogs. He quickly realised that attack was the best defence and he would dash forward with a rumbling snarl and snap at any dog who came near him. That usually saw them off, but if that didn't work, he'd learned to be fast on his paws and, being so small, could slip under low pieces of furniture to escape. He remembered his mother fondly, she'd nurtured him and his litter mates and taught them well until, one by one they had disappeared and then it was just the two of them. One day when Jack was distracted and shut in another room, his mother too had disappeared, leaving the small dog alone in the house with the other dogs and the single human. He had looked everywhere for her, calling her name and getting no response. Finally, he had ceased searching and his howls of despair had filled the house.

He turned to his friend, Norris, for comfort and distraction from his grief. Strictly speaking Norris was Jack's cousin, with similar breeding but Norris had turned out twice the size of Jack and with smooth tan fur. Norris had inherited two large Chi ears, as well as those bulgy Chi eyes, so was better placed for lookout duties. Jack and Norris got on well and soon they were sharing adventures and getting into scrapes together. Whenever the pack got too rowdy in the house and fighting took over, the human separated the dogs into cages. Jack and Norris shared, taking it in turns to chew at the wire cage and to scratch each other.

And the scratching! Ooooh that was better! The fleas hopped from dog to dog, sucking out blood and making them itchy. Jack rubbed his back on the cage bars and scratched his ears with his paws, but oh how he itched! Norris was the same, but they'd come to a scratch, itch, scratch understanding where they chewed and scratched each other's itchy spots in those hard to reach areas. That's what friends were for, after all.

This particular Monday started out like all the other days. The friends were sleeping in the sofa and Jack stretched and yawned and casually started to scratch at an ear. The old, green sofa in the living room had seen better days and over the years multiple dogs had chewed holes in it and ripped out the stuffing so that now there were spaces in between the springs where smaller dogs could slip to the safe spaces inside.

The sofa den was one of several dens the small dogs had made in the house. Dens were made out of cubby holes and narrow passages that a small dog could squeeze into, but a human or larger dog couldn't get to and the cats rarely came near. In the living room, there was the comfy chair - this was a matching chair to the sofa and, in the same way as the sofa, small dogs could wriggle through a hole between the springs and stuffing to a den inside. There was the place under the stairs, the space in the dingy hall behind the hall table with its boxes and piles of human stuff, you had to be small to squeeze under the table and fit through the gap in the wall. There was the space under the kitchen cupboards where a dog had chewed the corners of a plinth board and small dogs could slip behind. This was colder and with a hard concrete floor, but a small dog could enter at one end of the kitchen units and leave at the other, this den had the advantage of allowing dogs to cross the kitchen without being seen.

There could have been dens upstairs too, but the small dogs didn't venture up there often because of the cats. The cats ruled upstairs, cruel, vicious creatures with sharp claws that could catch and torture an unsuspecting small dog if that dog weren't careful. There were three of them and when they weren't sleeping or torturing some other creature, they lay in wait, tails twitching from side to side. Better to stay downstairs near the dens.

Outside was off-limits, dogs were not allowed to go out of the house. Monsters lurked out there, Jack was told, monsters who would gobble up small dogs who went out alone. Only the cats were allowed out and they slipped quickly and silently in and out through a gap in the window frame of the disintegrating conservatory at the back of the house. Cats, Jack knew, were well able to take care of themselves. They had razor sharp teeth and claws and they weren't slow to use them. Yes, cats were safe from monsters!

So, on this Monday morning and lying inside the sofa, Jack nudged Norris, "Wake up sleepy head! It's morning time, I think I can hear breakfast!"

Norris stretched out and opened one eye, "Steady on fella, can't a chap finish off his sleep in peace?" He closed his eye again.

Jack waved a paw excitedly, "Wake up, wake up now Norris!"

"Let me be," mumbled his friend, "I'm sleeping."

"You don't understand, Norris. I can smell meaty chunks! We must go at once!" and on this mysterious pronouncement, Jack started to wriggle out of the sofa.

Norris was wide awake now, "Meaty chunks! Well why didn't you say so? Get a move on, I'm coming!" and he followed Jack, wriggling his way out of the sofa.

Because Jack was so tiny, he slipped out of the sofa easily but it took Norris a bit of squeezing and lots of grunting before he could wriggle out of his hiding place, but soon he was free and he jumped off the sofa and both little dogs raced over the threadbare living room carpet and out towards the kitchen. They rounded the corner and Jack screeched to a halt, Norris bumping his nose into Jack's black-splodged bottom.

"Ow! What did you stop for?" hissed Norris as he started to rub his nose.

"Bigs!" came the cryptic reply, "Cairns and Bigs!" Even more cryptically now.

But Norris seemed to understand this. "Make for the den whilst their backs are turned!" he hissed and both dogs nipped across the edge of the tiled floor and around the chewed edge of the kitchen units, then disappeared under them. They edged along beneath the units, past previously scavenged and hidden items. They nudged their way past an old sock, an empty plastic bottle and some strips of material from an old fleece blanket which were mixed up with small piles of dog poo.

"Phew it's a bit whiffy under here this morning!" A third voice joined them. Another dog was already in the kitchen den and he quickly turned to look at them. George was another of their friends and he was nearly as small as Jack, but with ginger coloured, long, wiry hair and white paws.

"It's a tough one, the Bigs are already there waiting, and the Cairns are in prime positions, but we should get a chance," he continued, then turned his head back so he could see out from the far end of the den.

The Bigs he referred to were the big dogs. Huge, lumbering beasts that could crush or hurt a small dog with one careless turn or a push of their massive bodies. They weren't particularly nasty, but they held their own ground and their sheer size made them worthy of respect. The Cairns were the yappy, whiny, tell-on-you, alarm-sounding Cairn Terriers. Black and shaggy, they hung around in dark corners where they weren't noticed until too late. The minute they saw anything unusual they would set up a high-pitched, yapping noise which acted as an alert to the pack and they reported back to the Bigs about any misdemeanours or indiscretions made by the rest of the dogs. Small dogs bent on a food mission wanted to avoid notice by the Cairns and getting squashed or pushed by the Bigs.

"Hey now, we're nearly there!" George's nose twitched as he sniffed the air.

The human had been spooning great dollops of a meaty substance into an array of containers set out on the cluttered surfaces of the kitchen. The gravy oozed over the meaty chunks as they were ladled into the bowls and pots and onto plates and dishes of all sizes and colours. On the floor, and at the feet of the human, a seething pack of dogs, also of all sizes and colours, lay in wait. They watched expectantly as the great spoonfuls of juicy meat were put out on the worktop above their heads. Right-left, right-left, their eyes followed the spoon as it did its work until finally the human put the spoon down. This was it!

Now the human started to grab the bowls and plates and moved backwards into the sea of dogs to start to put them on the floor. As the first bowl was placed down, an ear-piercing shriek was let loose. A Cairn had sounded the breakfast alert, "Food! Food! Food!"

The Bigs jumped forward, pushing smaller dogs out of the way, shoving their mouths and noses into the bowls of food and gulping great mouthfuls up. Smaller dogs tried to push their way to the front as the human continued to put food down, but they were blocked and pushed out by the gluttonous Bigs time and time again.

The small dogs under the kitchen units were waiting, biding their time. And soon that moment came, a small plate was put down in the corner next to the unit and was pushed towards them by the gobbling, grabbing mass of dogs. George was swift, he reached his small nose out, opened his mouth and grabbed the plate with his teeth. He pulled with all his might then both he and the plate shot backwards under the units. Norris was keeping guard and repelled any noses that followed by the simple expedient of nipping them. "Ouch!" "Ow!" "Gerroff me!" The plan worked and soon the noses disappeared to find easier pickings.

The three small dogs sat looking at the plate. "Breakfast then!" announced Norris and sank his nose into a meaty morsel.

"Not yet! Not without Maisie," George shouted and bounded to the other end of the den to look out.

Norris stopped, mid-guzzle. "Maisie! I'd forgotten about Maisie," he said as he and Jack turned to watch George.

George peeked carefully out. At the back of the seething, swaying mass of dogs, a tiny, delicate cream Chihuahua was trying to push her way forward, but the bigger dogs were pushing her back and she kept being knocked off her feet. She would take a few valiant steps forward, then the pack would heave and she'd be back where she started.

"Maisie!" hissed George, "Over here!" and watched as she turned her head and saw him.

Maisie wagged her tail and tried to turn round. But the pack had other ideas, and it heaved over to the left, carrying Maisie with it, and for a short time she disappeared under the heaving mass of fur and tails.

"Maisie!" George shouted this time and started to bound forward, but the pack heaved once more and a small cream body shot out from under a pair of big black legs and landed at George's feet.

"You called?" Breathless and panting, but looking up at him with the most beautiful big brown eyes he'd ever seen, Maisie had arrived.

George gazed into those eyes. *If only...* he mused, as he looked down at her.

Giving himself a quick shake, he nudged her to her feet. "Follow me," he said as he led the way into the den and back to where his friends and the plate of food were waiting.

"Morning boys, have you started without me?" Maisie looked at Norris who had gravy dribbling down his chin and who shifted uncomfortably under her stare.

"Just a taster, you know."

"Well never mind, we're all here now, let's dig in." She waved a dainty paw at the dish and with that all the small dogs started to eat.

The dogs had different styles of eating, each according to their natures. Maisie was delicate but methodical, she firstly selected a meaty chunk, licked the gravy off it, then chewed the chunk in half to eat it. Norris just guzzled, he pushed his nose in and with great gulps ate his way through the nearest pile of food. George was thorough and efficient, he started at one side of the plate and chewed his way systematically through the pile of food. But Jack was different. A bit of a grazer at best, he hated to eat with the other dogs, he worried they might steal his food or hurt him. It was a feeling he couldn't shake, even when here with his friends. So, one by one, Jack removed meaty chunks from the plate and took them over to the other corner where he steadily chewed his way through them.

Slowly the pile of meaty chunks on the plate reduced as the four small dogs ate, each in their own special way, until finally there was only a smear of gravy left, which Norris lapped up before licking his lips with a satisfied sigh.

"Well I do declare, that was some feast!" He sat back to give his back leg a quick chew with his teeth. The food had warmed him up making his flea bites itch.

"Yum!" agreed Jack, who was still chewing a small chunk of meat that had got stuck in his teeth. He finally swallowed it, "So Maisie, what were you doing out there? Surely you know the Bigs won't let you through?"

"I know, but I was so hungry and I didn't see you boys and Max told me the food was out and perhaps I should try to grab some...." Her voice trailed off as she caught sight of George who had quickly raised his head at her words.

"Max told you what?" he asked grimly, "Maisie, you know he can't be trusted, I've told you before."

"I forgot and I was so hungry and thought that maybe, just maybe I could try. But the Bigs were just so..." She waved a paw, ".... so big, I suppose, and I battled and battled." She looked shyly up at George's face, "Then I looked up and you rescued me."

"Well, I suppose there's no harm done." Gruffly now, he continued, "Maisie you need to be careful in future, Max can't be trusted."

Jack chimed in, "He's right you know Maisie, Max tells you lies, he likes to cause trouble. He's not your friend."

Maisie looked sad, her big brown eyes looked searchingly round her friends and her nose quivered, "He seemed so genuine though, I thought it'd be alright. He was right beside me and then I lost sight of him when the Bigs started pushing…" her voice trailed off again. "I messed up, didn't I?"

Under her soulful gaze all three of her friends crumbled, shuffled their paws and muttered excuses, "Not really Maisie." "You didn't know." "It's not your fault."

For a minute silence reigned as each small dog reflected on the matter. Maisie always gave more attention than she should to

Max, but then Max could be very persuasive. A handsome cockapoo, with sleek black glossy curls, he turned all the girls' heads. With a quick tongue and ready compliments, he could talk them into daring exploits which somehow never benefited them as much as it did Max. And then, when things got hairy, as they inevitably did, Max always managed to slip away only to later laugh it off if his victim complained. "You must have misunderstood me? Why did you think I told you to do that?" Oh yes, her friends knew Max's tricks alright and they also knew Maisie's enormous, kind, caring heart and gullible nature which led her into trouble.

Then finally Norris, never one to be sad or sorry for long, broke the silence. "Well, never mind all that now, we need to have a plan for today. I've heard there's a council meeting later and we need to be prepared."

"Council meeting? We'd better get organised. Jack, we'll need your help there then, you must have heard some things?" George had been looking glum, but the announcement by Norris spurred him into action. "What's on the agenda tonight then Norris?"

"The usual stuff y'know, a reminder of the house rules, the Cairns will tell us who's been breaking which ones and then there'll be the allocation of punishments. Then we'll have the reselection of officials - it'll be the same old faces, no change there. But there is one new agenda item under 'Any Other Business', the cats are introducing it."

"What's that then Norris?" Maisie looked at him enquiringly.

"Well I'm not really sure, it just says 'Visitors' with no other explanation."

The friends agreed this sounded puzzling, so George took the lead. "Jack, you keep your ear to the ground and see if you can find out anything, we've got until this evening to see if we need to take action, make sure you keep us all informed. Now, has anyone got anything to fear from the Cairns report?"

They all shook their heads, luckily they'd been good at evading notice this month, but it wasn't always that way. And if they hadn't been noticed, then some other poor dog would have fallen foul of the Cairns and would be dragged in front of the council to answer for their sins. Someone had to be punished each month in order to keep the fear going which fed the control by the few over the many in the house.

The few were the elected dog officials who were nearly all the Bigs and they ruled the house primarily because they could push and shove the smaller dogs around. Not blessed with much intellect, they ruled by fear, and public punishments for misdemeanours was one such mechanism. They were supported by a series of sneaky clingers-on, like the Cairns who acted as policemen and others who worked as informers. Max, the small dogs suspected, was one such informer.

Oh yes, the small dogs knew how the council worked and also how it paid off to be prepared. But for now there were more pressing concerns. "I'm thirsty! Have they finished yet?" Norris motioned with his head towards the kitchen where the sounds of the pack scrabbling and fighting over breakfast had been slowly quietening down.

"I'll check, wait a moment." Jack quickly popped his nose around the edge of the plinth to take a look. The kitchen was now empty of dogs, except for one golden spaniel who was vainly trying to lick under one of the mass of empty bowls left behind on the floor. "There's only Toby left, and he's a friend," he reported. "I'll need to speak with him, he gets to know things."

The small dogs quietly crept out of their den and made their way over to a large beige dish which was half full of water. "Go on Maisie, boys, you drink first, " offered George, "I'll keep watch."

And so three of the small dogs drank their fill whilst the small ginger dog stood lookout, his tail up, his eyes bright and his ginger moustache bristling. When they'd had their fill, it was his turn and he lapped up the cool water thirstily. "That's better," he said, "Jack, we'll leave you to talk with Toby."

With that, three of the small dogs made their way out of the kitchen, the boys stopping at the doorway to sniff and cock their back legs and leaving Jack sitting by the water bowl watching Toby who was still hopefully licking at all the plates and bowls. "Hi Toby, what news?"

Chapter Two

Toby stopped his licking and sat back "Oh hi Jack, where'd you all come from so suddenly?" He'd seen them appear by the water bowl but had taken little notice because he was trying to get a last scrap of meat from under a plate. He wasn't really that surprised, he knew the small dogs could often squeeze into spaces where a larger dog couldn't go and was quite used to them popping up all over the place.

"We used the Run," Jack moved closer to the bigger dog. "Got ourselves some breakfast. How about you? I hear there's a meeting tonight, any news?"

"Sure is, and think I'm for the high jump! The Cairns caught me last week. Bit of a pain really, but you know how it is, I just wasn't careful enough."

Jack had already heard on the dog grapevine that Toby had been caught going outside and that the Cairns were reporting him. What he didn't know was why Toby had let himself be caught, he was usually more careful.

"How did that happen, Toby? I thought you took care?"

"Well, you know, I was talking to Max, and he was telling me about the cats' proposed item for the meeting tonight, when all of a sudden I remembered Postie. Well after that, it was done and dusted in a blur, but of course Cairns had seen me, hadn't they?"

Jack nodded. Fortunately he was quite aware of Toby's love of chasing the postman so he could make sense of this confusing speech. Slowly he got the muddled story out of him.

Toby, it seemed, had been distracted from his usual position at the front door at the time the postman called. The door had been opened so the human could receive and sign for a large, official looking letter, and Toby had noticed rather late the fact that a stranger was standing in their midst. With a huge "Woof!" he had sprung forward, past the human and chased poor Postie out of the porch and down the path in front of the house until Postie had more or less vaulted the front gate to get away.

Postie had stood the other side of the front wall whilst Toby ran up and down the garden side, barking at the unwanted stranger. "You cheeky so and so, you," had panted Postie, "but they'll be coming for you now, the whole darned lot of you!" Then he had hoisted his post bag further onto his shoulder and stomped away.

After a few more gusty barks at the retreating back of his enemy, Toby had turned and slunk back towards the front door of the house. The human had stood silently whilst he passed, but he had seen Max and the Cairns slink away.

Jack had been listening with his head on one side, his Chi ear turned to Toby. "Do you think Max set you up, Toby? There'll be a price to pay now the Cairns have seen you, they're bound to report that you went outside."

Toby sighed. "I know it's not allowed, but it just happened and that Postie, well he needed to be taught a lesson. Max was just talking to me, I can't blame him. I haven't told anyone else, but what do you think Postie meant, Jack?"

Jack frowned. "I don't know, but I'd keep it to yourself, it can't do you any good if they find out an outsider spoke to you."

Toby nodded, his glossy golden ears bouncing slowly up and down with his head. "I know, I'm going to say nothing tonight, they think I'm stupid and only interested in chasing things anyway. I'm more interested in what the cats are going to say. Max didn't finish but he said they were going to talk about visitors, I think he said visitors to the house, but we got interrupted." With this he resumed his licking of plates. "You'd think they'd leave something for me, I'm starving!"

"It's always the same, the bigger, pushier dogs get the food first and we smaller, weaker dogs get left with nothing," said Jack bitterly. "Would cat crunchies help?"

"I'd eat anything, but how can we get cat crunchies, the cats will never share them?"

"Ah, well if you're very small and have a tongue like mine, then there are ways, come!" Jack led Toby over to a small gap between the kitchen units and the fridge. Now Jack was well known for having a tiny nose but an exceptionally long tongue and this unique combination allowed him to lick and pull things out from tiny gaps. He now stuck his nose into the gap and started to flick out cat crunchies with his tongue.

"Mmmm!" mumbled Toby as he caught and chewed them, "Mmmm, mmmm they're good!" He swallowed several large mouthfuls of them before the supply ran out. "Thanks Jack, that should help. How come they were there?"

"The cats get fed on the work surface above and knock them over the edge when they argue. They haven't got long tongues and won't stay long on the floor in case of dogs, so they leave them. It's my emergency store room for small dogs, so I can help my friends." Jack said proudly, "It's the best I can do."

"Well, they've hit the spot with me in any case. You're a good friend, Jack. Now I'll just get a drink, will you keep watch for me?"

"Of course." Jack knew how all the smaller dogs felt vulnerable at the water bowl. They had to have their heads and ears down and the noise made by the lapping meant that someone could sneak up behind them. The cats were very good at this, and they had nasty, unpredictable tempers which often meant anyone in their way got a swipe with their sharp claws. So the tiny white dog sat down and watched carefully, with his Chi ear up and his Jack ear to the side as his larger friend took a long drink, golden ears bouncing in time with his lapping. To anyone watching the effect was comical, but a seriousness underlay the event, and Toby quickly finished, then both dogs parted ways.

"Thanks again, Jack, I'll see you tonight." Toby trotted off out of the kitchen towards the hall where he liked to keep watch on the front door.

Jack decided to make his way out via the Run. He had some tidying up to do first. He headed for the gap in the plinth and had just wriggled under the units when he heard voices coming into the kitchen. He didn't think they had seen him so he lay down quietly in the gloom and listened.

"Stupid Toby, there he goes, hoping to chase Postie again!" Jack recognised the high pitched shriek of Sue, one of the Cairns, and lay even lower.

"Yes but we've got a witness and we'll make our report, he'll be for it at the meeting tonight." The other, slightly lower, voice was Stu, her brother. "I don't think much damage was done, and of course we'll ask him tonight, but we can't have dogs disobeying the rules, especially at this time. We'll press for maximum punishment, the Bigs will understand."

Jack heard sounds of them crossing the floor, then lapping the water. "Best get back to duty then, keep your eyes peeled Sue." Then the sounds of footsteps receded as the Cairns left the kitchen.

What did they mean by "especially at this time", pondered Jack. He couldn't work it out. It was like a giant puzzle and he was slowly collecting the pieces, but he couldn't yet fit them together. With a shrug, he started to tidy up the den. He picked up a couple of dishes that were under the units and pushed them outside then he lay down for a while thoughtfully chewing the old sock that lay on the floor. Jack liked to chew small, soft items, it helped him to think. *There's something really dodgy going on here and I'm going to find out what,* he decided. With that, he made his way along the den, stopping briefly at the end to quickly scan for any threats, then crossed the short piece of open floor and made his way out of the kitchen, pausing at the doorway to sniff and cock his little leg as his friends had done earlier.

Jack made his way to the dining room. If it looked safe he wanted to lie in the sun that sometimes streamed in through the patio doors. Today he was in luck, there was no sign of Bigs or Cairns, just a myriad selection of small and medium dogs lounging around, occasionally scratching and turning around but mostly sleeping. He spied the place he was aiming for, an empty spot on the door ledge just behind the curtain and in full glorious sun. He nipped over to it, dodging the snoring bodies of the other dogs and settled down to have a doze in the warmth.

He slept fitfully, in his dream he was being chased by something, something large that wanted to get him. He was chased through the rooms of the house and even up the stairs. Now he didn't want to go upstairs because of the cats, but he was scared. He reached the top of the stairs and the large thing caught up with him. It reached out and grabbed hold of him, dragging him backwards and then it shook him… *"No, no, no!"*

He was being shaken, but it was back in real life now and he opened his eyes.

"Jack, Jack, wake up!" It was Elsie the black and tan Dachshund and she was looking down at him with concern in her eyes as she tugged at his fur to wake him.

"Wha... what?" Jack was confused, his brain was still reeling from his nightmare and his body was shaking with fear.

"Wake up Jack, you were screaming!" Elsie sat back now that she had his attention.

Jack shook his head slowly as if to shake away the horrid dreams. He was glad it was Elsie who'd woken him, she was one of the good ones, one of the ones he could trust. "Sorry Elsie, bit of a nightmare, I didn't mean to scare you."

"You were shouting that you had to get away from something, something that was coming to get you. What did you mean, Jack?" Elsie was always the knowing one, intuitive and she could read him like a book. Jack shrugged but she gazed into his eyes and he wondered fir a moment whether she could read his thoughts. But she shook her head and said simply, "You've had too much sun, Jack. Best get out of the heat, come follow me."

He followed her now, her long back swaying over impossibly tiny legs as she wove her way through the legs of the dining room table until they came to a chair in a quiet corner, away from the other dogs. They sat down beneath it and she turned to him and whispered, "Have you heard the rumours?"

Jack kept his voice low too. "What rumours, Elsie?"

"I've been hearing things, little snippets of stuff, but can't quite put it together. When you started shouting like that I thought you must know something, because it sounded just like..." her voice trailed off and she sat staring anxiously at the wall for a moment. "Well, it sounded like Max." She quickly glanced at him as she saw him stiffen, Jack knew she was sweet on Max, who with his handsome face and smooth talk charmed all of the girls. "Yes I know he lies, but he was talking to Sue and Stu and they didn't know I was there, so I think it was true. Max said that there would be visitors to the house and that they would be inspecting any animals they found. He said they had to get most of the dogs to disappear when the visitors came so only the Bigs were seen and they could put on a good show. The best way to do this was to scare the other dogs, he said, he called it the *fear project*. I wondered if you'd heard those rumours too?"

"I've only heard a few snippets, Toby told me Postie said something about them coming for us and I heard Stu tell Sue that they'd press for maximum punishment for Toby to ensure the dogs obey the rules. Elsie, he said, *'especially at this time'*. There's something going on and I don't trust them." Jack was worried too.

"I'd heard about Toby going outside, I didn't know that Postie had said anything to him, he'll need to be careful the Bigs don't find out." Elsie's large brown eyes looked concerned. Her ears flicked up as she heard a dog approaching, "Time we were moving on, Jack, don't want to draw attention," and she walked off towards the door to the hall.

Jack waited a moment for her to leave the room and then he too walked out into the hall, by the time he got there, Elsie had disappeared.

As Jack entered the hall his friend Norris bounded up to him. Norris had, he said, been coming to look for him because he'd found something he would be interested in. If Jack would just follow him, Norris would show him. His interest piqued, Jack followed Norris over to the space under the stairs. Norris motioned with his head, "Look Jack, between the wall and the boxes, look at what the cats have dropped!"

Jack squeezed his head into the gap and saw the small object that had fallen down from the landing upstairs. A small, grey furry item with a long tail was wedged just beyond his reach.

"It's a toy, Jack, use your tongue!" urged Norris.

Jack opened his mouth and stretched out his long, pink tongue till he could just feel the fur with it. He wriggled his head a bit more, then managed to wrap his tongue around the tail of the toy and pull it out.

Both dogs stood staring down at a small grey, furry mouse toy that smelt a bit strange. "It's a catnip mouse," said Norris, "I heard the cats say they'd lost it and I could smell but not quite reach it."

"Ha! It's a toy, and it's ours now," laughed Jack and he jumped on top of it and, grabbing it quickly with his teeth, shook it from side to side.

"Grrrrr!" he snarled as he jumped up and down, shaking and biting the toy, whilst Norris looked on, laughing. "Take that, toy!" he growled as he pounded his little paws on it. The mouse was tossed around, unseeing and unblinking.

The small commotion made a small head pop out from the den under the stairs. "What's going on?" asked George as he watched Norris start to join in the fun by pouncing on the toy whilst Jack held one end. Soon the friends began a slow tug-of-war, with both small dogs pulling with all their might, one at each end of the toy mouse. "Oh, I see, it's a game! Maisie, come and see what Jack and Norris are playing with," he said, and another cream head popped out to watch.

Soon all four of the small dogs were out in the hall, enjoying the game. They played happily together, taking it in turns to pounce on then shake the small toy, or to throw it in the air and catch it. Sometimes two of the dogs would join in together and pull at the same time in a tug-of-war. There was lots of laughing and fake growling, but the whole thing was a good natured game with the small dogs playing enthusiastically.

Slowly, a small crowd of onlookers appeared. Firstly Toby, then Elsie, then several of the other house dogs joined the throng, choosing to cheer on the small dogs in their game, but not get involved. With the growling coming from the small dogs as they played with the toy and the cheering on from the onlookers, the noise level steadily rose. One dog quietly slunk away, off to warn others.

The game was progressing well and Jack and George this time were engaged in the tug-of-war. Jack had his teeth firmly attached to the head end of the toy, had dug in his small white paws and was pulling with all his might at one end. At the other end George had hold of the tail and had locked his ginger legs into a similar pattern and was equally tugging away with all of his strength. The two were equally matched, so the duel went on for several minutes.

"Grrrrr!" growled Jack between clenched teeth as he tried a series of fast tugs on the mouse.

"Grrrr-rrrrr!" growled George as he hung on and tried a number of counter tugs on his end.

"Grrrr-grrr-arrrr!" snapped and snarled a new voice as an enormous black and tan dog leapt into the middle snatching the small toy away from the small dogs and holding it aloft. Magnificent and massive, Sidney the Doberman was one of the Bigs and he towered over the small dogs. "Enough of this fooling around and making noise!" he growled savagely through clenched teeth. "You know toys aren't allowed!" With that, he ground his massive teeth on the catnip mouse, and quickly shredded it. "Pfft!" he spat out the shredded material and stuffing. "Let that be a lesson to you all, no disobedience!" he growled and strode off, with pounding, purposeful steps out of the hall.

The small dogs stood and stared after him. Little Maisie who, seconds before, had been loving the game, went up to the shredded pieces of the toy and put her nose into them. "He's ruined it!" she cried and there were real tears welling up in her soft brown eyes. Why must the Bigs destroy everything we love?" and she sat down with a whimper.

The onlookers slowly filtered away until it was just her friends left to console her. George went over and placed his nose on her shoulder, "Don't cry Maisie, we'll find another toy. We'll just have to play where the Bigs can't get to us."

"Yeah, and play quietly so they can't hear us, and don't have too many to join in so that nobody gets to know about it, what fun is that?" she asked, bitterly.

"I don't know Maisie, but we'll find a way somehow. Come dry your tears, we'll pop into the den and I'm sure Jack will have some news to tell us."

"It's true, I have a bit of news, but I'm not sure what it all means. Come, we'll talk in the den." Jack nodded and the friends crawled into the space under the stairs, where he told them about the things he'd heard that day.

The rest of the day was spent scavenging for more food, sleeping and generally scratching each other. At tea time there was a brief kerfuffle when the human put down dry dog food. As there was plenty put down, and in more places, it tended to be scattered more widely by the bigger, greedy dogs and so the smaller dogs could grab mouthfuls and retreat to safer places to eat it.

Once tea was served and eaten, the challenge for the dogs was not to be caught by the human. Any dogs who were caught arguing or causing damage by chewing house items were locked up in the dog cages overnight. These were piled up in the dining room, wire cages with no blankets or other softness to lie on and no access to food, water or a means to relieve yourself. It was a long uncomfortable night in the cages but fortunately for the small dogs, tonight they were lying quietly in the den under the stairs and so avoided the lockdown.

Chapter Three

Tuesday dawned and started, as most mornings did, with the human coming downstairs, followed by the three cats, Izzy, Lizzy and Kizzy. The cats went straight over to the gap in the window frame and escaped outside, no doubt to savage a Monster or two! The human switched on the kettle in the kitchen and started to open up the cages and release the dogs from their overnight imprisonment. The house sounds rose as dogs stretched, scratched and greeted each other, small scuffles breaking out as dogs trod on each other and made their way to favourite sniffing places and scratching doorways, table legs and pieces of furniture on the way.

No meaty chunks for breakfast this morning but the human refilled the water bowls and scattered more dry dog food and even several biscuits around so it was a quieter and fairer breakfast for all. Cat food was put out on the work surfaces for the three cats who returned from outside, sniffed it suspiciously and swiped any careless dog nose that came near with a sharp claw.

This morning, although Toby waited expectantly in the hall, there was no visit from Postie who, instead of risking the wrath of the dogs, walked nonchalantly past, whistling as he went.

The dog council meeting was that evening and most of the day was spent in expectation of it. There was a low buzz of excited chatter between all the dogs as they waited for the time to be right. The usual small flare ups of minor grumbles arose when dogs argued over warm spots to lie in and whose turn at the water bowl it was, but mainly the day dragged quietly on in suppressed expectation.

As evening approached, so did the time of the council. Once more the human fed the animals and then sat to enjoy her own tea and placed the dishes in the kitchen. Then, at the appointed time, the signal came. The telephone in the living room rang and the human shooed all the dogs out of that room, closed the door, sat down in the easy chair and picked up the receiver to talk to her sister.

That was the signal for the council to start. "Council! Council! Take your places!" shrieked Sue and Stu as they bullied and mustered all the dogs into the dining room. In that room, the officials were already in position. In front of the patio doors and with the low evening sun shining through behind them the Bigs sat at the front, facing their audience. Sidney the Doberman and the biggest of the Bigs, sat at dead centre and was flanked to his right by Ruby, a portly but very determined chocolate Labrador and to his left by Titan, a brindle Staffordshire Bull Terrier, the 'muscle' of the group.

To the left of the Bigs sat the three cats, and the space on their other side was reserved for the Cairns once the mustering of the rest of the dogs was complete. "Hurry now, latecomers will be punished!" snarked Sue and to prove her point snapped at the heels of a tardy Yorkshire Terrier, causing her to yelp in surprise but to quicken her pace.

"Twenty nine, thirty, thirty one," counted Stu, "yes that's all accounted for now." He pushed the dining room door closed, joining Sue at the front of the room with the Bigs and the cats. They faced the rows of other dogs who were quietly lined up, waiting for the meeting to start.

"Thirty one?" asked Maisie, under her breath, "I thought we were thirty two last time, who's missing?" But the small dogs shook their heads, they didn't seem to know and nobody could recall anyone saying that a dog had disappeared.

"Right, let the meeting start then," said Sidney as he surveyed the rows of expectant faces in front of him. "As usual, I will ask Stu to start his report on discipline and obedience with a quick run through the rules."

"Yes, Sir!" and Stu started to reel off a list of rules that the dogs weren't quite following properly, these were mostly humdrum with the odd reminder here and there of what the dogs should be doing. "Rule Five: Toys - the playing with." He paused, stared hard at the small dogs, then continued, "Some dogs were caught playing with a toy. I believe you, Sir, witnessed and dealt with this one yourself?"

"Yes!" Sidney frowned as he picked up the theme. "May I remind everyone that no toys or items pertaining to be toys may be played with, unless officially sanctioned by this council. This is to keep all dogs safe as toys may be dangerous to dogs." He paused for effect, then with his sharp ears standing tall and his teeth bared he glared at all the dogs as he continued, "Why only this week I stopped a game with a cat toy that contained POISONOUS catnip. The safety of all dogs is paramount to the dog council and this is why we have these rules." Sidney watched the faces of the assembled dogs carefully for any sign of dissent, but the dogs had been to these meetings before and knew that to be singled out was dangerous, so they kept quiet, eyes cast down. "I believe that the immediate action I carried out should serve as punishment enough, but I think the dogs should make sure they remember this rule better. So, Stu, can you lead the repeat on this one?"

Stu, puffing out his shaggy chest at this opportunity to excel, barked out loudly, "Thank you Sir! Right everyone, repeat after me: Toys are dangerous and may not be played with!"

The assembled dogs, as a group, repeated the rule, keeping their eyes fixed either on the floor or straight ahead, but nobody caught each other's eye. The cats, meanwhile, smirked between themselves, also taking care not to catch Sidney's eye.

"Right, Stu, next!"

"Rule 6: Outside - the venturing beyond the house." Stu puffed out his shaggy chest once more. "Last week, Sir, a dog was seen going outside! Outside Sir!" He puffed his chest out even further, such was his indignation at the flouting of this rule, "This was a flagrant breach of this rule and cannot be allowed to pass without action!"

"Who was the perpetrator? Bring them forward now!" Sidney barked.

At this point, Toby, who had been sitting trembling at the front of the crowd, was pushed forward by Sue, until he sat facing the officials and with his back to the other dogs. "Here he is Sir! Toby is the culprit!" she told them.

"Now, now," intervened Ruby swiftly. She had been listening carefully and now raised her fat body up and leant forward to wave a front paw as she made her point. "Sue, we don't want to *lead* proceedings, after all we want a fair trial for this crime. Toby is the *accused*," she emphasised.

"Good point, Ruby, thanks for putting us right," oozed Sidney. "We want to treat all dogs fairly as you all know. Sue, you will address Toby as the accused in future."

The assembled dogs sat, impassive still. This too they had all heard before. The facade of the trial, the play acting of fairness, the rules that supposedly kept them safe but made no sense, the punishments for dissent, yes they'd witnessed these many times before. So they sat, quietly and motionless and let the story unfold.

"Ahem!" coughed Stu, "Right, well the *accused* stands, erm... er... stands well er... accused of going outside on Wednesday last week, contrary to rule six and without good reason. This misdemeanour was witnessed by one witness and, indeed, Sue and myself when he returned to the house."

"Indeed," Sidney stared grimly at Toby, "What do you have to say in this matter?"

Toby was shaking, "Well Sid, sorry, Sir, I, er, sorry..." he trailed off.

"See , Sir, he's guilty and can't even answer the charge," piped up Sue, her ears and tail bristling with indignation at this transgression.

"Let him speak," once more Ruby leaned her corpulent body forward as she intervened. "Come on Toby," she coaxed, "why did you do such a thing? What were you thinking of going outside?"

"Well, Ma'am, it was Postie you see..." Toby met Ruby's eye and started to recount his story. "I was just talking with Max and I got distracted, then all of a sudden the front door was open and Postie was standing there. Well, Ma'am, you know how I feel about strangers, so I chased him out and he ran away. That's all there was to it really."

"I see," replied Ruby. "Did you also see or hear anything outside?"

"No, nothing, just Postie running away, and then I came back. It was all over so quick you see." Toby knew better than to divulge the words Postie had uttered, it would only get worse for him.

"That's right, well thank you for telling us your story, I'll hand back to Sidney now," Ruby nodded to her colleague.

Sidney was looking grimmer than ever, "In that case, Toby, you know I have to find you guilty of breaking one of our most important rules. As you are well aware, the rules are in place to protect us all and keep us safe. By going outside you put everyone at risk from the monsters who live out there. This misbehaviour cannot be ignored and must be punished. Have you got anything further to add?"

"No, Sir, I, it was just a mistake," said Toby lamely, shaking from head to toe with fear.

Sidney looked to his right and left, Ruby and Titan nodded, "We are in agreement then, the punishment will be one slash on the nose and two nights spent in solitary confinement. Titan, cats, step forward if you please?"

At this command, Titan and the three cats stepped forward. Titan stood on the other side of Toby from Sue, blocking his escape and then opened his big jaws to grab Toby by the scruff of his neck. Toby, thus immobilised, stood waiting for the cats. The three cats slunk forward and stood in a line in front of Toby. He rolled his eyes in fear, waiting.

"Do it!" commanded Sidney.

Lightning fast, a paw flashed out from the cats, so fast that nobody could see which cat it belonged to. This was the idea of course, no recriminations could be made for the act of punishment if dogs didn't know which cat had actually struck. It also kept the poor victim guessing until the last moment and lessened the chance of them flinching, the paw missing and thus having the embarrassment of repeating the punishment. Out of the cat huddle a paw quickly flashed and it drew a long, deep scratch down Toby's nose.

"Ow-wow-wow!" he howled as a stream of blood started to well on his nose as the cats hissed and spat at him then filed back to their spaces, punishment carried out.

Titan released his hold to walk back to his place facing all the dogs. "Let that be a lesson to you," he growled in Toby's ear as he turned.

"Let that be noted by all dogs, going outside will not be tolerated. Our friends, the cats, warn us about the monsters outside almost daily and we must keep each other safe." Sidney nodded in the cats' direction and they nodded back smugly in agreement. "Toby, Titan will supervise your confinement, starting tonight. Any further disobedience will not be tolerated by this council, I hope you have learned your lesson. You may retake your place with the others, the council has further things to discuss."

Toby slunk back into the ranks of the other dogs and sat down, wiping his sore, bleeding nose with his front paw until his sleek, golden fur turned a blood red. Elsie the Dachshund, who was next to him, moved closer, not making any big movements that could be detected by the Bigs, but just enough so that he could feel her body heat, warming him up and soothing his trembling and shaking. He kept his eyes to the front but relaxed his body towards hers, soaking up the warmth of a friend.

Chapter Four

Meanwhile, with the animals back in their allotted places, Sidney had moved on. In a great show of equality the council discussed more mundane items such as food allocation and duty rota for guarding the smaller dogs from dangers in the house. Although they remained silent, the other dogs weren't fooled. They knew there was no equality, just an iron one-sided rule by the Bigs and their supporters with a nod to fairness. A fairness which was never actually enacted at mealtimes and danger points, being instead a way of increasing observance and control. The smaller dogs often managed to get around these restrictions in their own way and by working together. They knew from past, bitter experience, there was little point in challenging the authority of the Bigs in the dog council so now they sat, mutely listening as Sidney continued.

"Item 4: Any Other Business," he stated. "I see we have a request to discuss visitors here, the cats are to present it. Well, cats, what's this all about?"

Izzy, the lead cat of the three, stepped forward. Sleek and glossy, her black coat glistened in the rays of the evening sun that shone through the patio doors. Her green eyes swept around the room to check she had everyone's attention. The dogs dutifully watched her, trying to evince a level of interest they didn't really feel. They were certain a rehashing of advice was due, in that they were to be exhorted to behave properly towards visitors (such as Postie) who called at the door and to make sure to let the officials handle it.

But Izzy startled them all with her next words. "We are expecting visitors to the house this week. We don't know how many, but we have received information that a number of visitors will be coming. We know that these visitors will be coming inside and inspecting both the house and the animals and we want to be prepared."

"Coming inside?" gasped Elsie. "Actual visitors?" She was still warming Toby up and forgot herself by speaking out loud.

"Yeess, the visitorsss will be cominggg inssside," another voice purred. Lizzie, a longer haired version of Izzy, joined in. She drew out the sounds of the words in a lisping, drawling way, typical of the cats. "We have it on good authorityyy you know. From our sssssources."

Elsie, resigned now to having made herself a target for recriminations, pressed on, "But we never have visitors inside the house, how can you be sure?"

"Sssources," responded the third cat, Kizzy, a smaller black cat than her friends, with white tipped nose and paws. "We have our sssources, more we cannot tell you."

"Hhhmph! Sources? That's not very helpful? How can we believe you if you can't reveal your sources?" Elsie was rattled now and forgetting herself by querying the cats' statements. A low rumble of mutterings swept through the other dogs as she did so.

"Silence!" barked Sidney, glaring at Elsie and waiting for the rumble to stop. "The meeting will come to order! Stu, do we have any other reports on this matter?"

"Certainly Sir, yes Sir! I have reports that corroborate what the cats are saying. Witness statements from overhearing what the human said to the Postie and on the telephone to her sister, Sir."

"There you go," replied Sidney. "We have witness statements as well."

Valiantly Elsie continued her argument, "But who are these witnesses Sir? What are their names, can we trust them?"

Sidney looked enquiringly at Stu whereupon a number of dogs at the back, Max among them, shuffled their paws and looked down at the floor. Stu simply responded that he couldn't divulge names for "operational reasons".

Sidney glared at Elsie one last time, "No more of these questions. We have the reports and now we must decide what actions we should take. I won't tolerate any more questions on this subject."

Elsie knew when she was beaten. "Yes Sir" she said dejectedly and cast her eyes down.

"So, tell me, cats," said Sidney, "what do we need to do?"

"Well, I've checked with other cats in the neighbourhood and they tell me that the visitors will likely be checking for dogs and looking at the house," purred Izzy as she stretched out and turned up her paw to study her claws.

"Yesss, they'll take dogssss away if they are not ssssatisfied with the conditionssss," added Lizzie, tail twitching anxiously.

"So, you'll need a plan to hide some of the dogs and tidy the place up," said Izzy, studiously licking her paw, one sharp claw at a time.

"Sounds like we need to get organised then." Sidney looked at the Cairns, "Stu and Sue, I'm going to make you responsible for arrangements. We need to have a reception committee for the visitors. That'll be Ruby, Titan and myself of course, as council officials. We'll need hiding places for all the other dogs and a tidy up session in the house to put away all the mess where it can't be seen. Naturally, the visitors should only be allowed in the living room."

"Yes Sir, we can organise that." Sue slyly added, "We will need your authority to do the necessary works, of course."

"Yes, yes, whatever it takes, we must be prepared!" Sidney blustered.

"Ahem," coughed Elsie, once more preparing herself to challenge. "Sir, why is all this necessary again and why are you giving the Cairns this power over us? Is there really such a threat?" she asked. There was a general rumbling of questioning remarks beside her.

"Yeah, why are we doing this?" asked another voice at the back.

For one moment Sidney looked as if he was going to explode, he lashed his tail in anger and spoke through his gleaming white teeth, "Impertinence! I will not allow it! No questioning of council decisions is allowed!" Then he lowered his tail and added, this time choosing his words more carefully, "Here we are, making a plan for keeping all the dogs safe from this threat and you ask these questions. The cats have made it clear that we are in danger, why dogs could be *taken away,* and we have set out a clear way forward to stop this happening. Really, you put all the dogs at risk with your questioning. It must stop now!"

Titan had stood up at the first rumblings in the ranks. He was a broad and well built dog with a wide chest and rippling muscles. He now walked up to Elsie and sniffed her face, "Take care, Elsie," he whispered. She cast her eyes down as he towered over her. Titan walked along the front row of dogs, his powerful jaws just inches away from their faces and they all lowered their eyes, nobody wanted to be singled out for attention. He returned to his place and sat down, carefully watching the rows of dogs.

"That's better! Ruby, do you have anything to add?" Sidney looked at his fellow official.

Ruby opened her eyes from her daydream and shifted her weight, "I just wanted to thank all the dogs now for the effort they will be putting in this week and to let them know that if they feel worried about anything they can bring any of their concerns to me."

The dogs, impassive now, with their gazes firmly fixed on the floor, had heard it all before. Ruby always made these offers, alluding to concern for the welfare of the dogs. However, they all knew from past experience that any dog who asked for help would be shrugged off and worse, was likely to be reported to Sidney and come more firmly under the scrutiny of Stu and Sue.

"Elsie, thank you for your question, I can talk privately after if you would like." Ruby said, smiling. But the smile didn't quite reach her ears.

Elsie, already beginning to regret her outburst, kept her eyes down and muttered, "No, it's okay. Really, I have my answer."

Sidney narrowed his eyes, but Elsie stood quietly, eyes down. "Well, that's sorted then. That was the final agenda item, so I declare the meeting finished, please leave in single file. Toby don't forget to report to Stu before it goes dark for your confinement."

With this, Sue walked over to the door, hooked a paw round it, and pulled it open. The Bigs left first, followed by the cats and then some of the other dogs and finally Sue and Stu. Finally, just a few of the smaller dogs were left in the middle of the room.

Chapter Five

"Come, it's not safe to talk here, someone may return," said George, looking at the worried faces around him. "We can squeeze into the den under the stairs - yes even you, Elsie. Let's go there now, I think we need our own plan." The small dogs filed over to the door, and one by one checked that the hall was clear before they quickly crossed it and wriggled through the space behind the boxes and into the den under the stairs. Norris went first, followed by Jack and then Maisie. Next, George watched as Elsie crossed the floor and wriggled her long body hard through the small gap until she reached the other side. Finally, George made one last check and scurried over and into the den.

The space inside the den was cosy and warm with five small dogs in there, but they would be safe from bigger dogs and prying eyes and ears. They sat in the darkness whilst their eyes adjusted to the lack of light.

"Wow, Elsie, you stuck your neck out in the meeting, you were so brave!" gasped Jack. He was secretly both proud and a bit envious of her courage as he knew he wouldn't have dared to speak up in front of the Bigs. But then Jack was a very tiny dog, the smallest of them all, and he knew that retribution could be taken slowly over time. Bigger dogs could push past or sit carelessly on a tiny dog and he could be hurt painfully in many sly ways with a series of "accidents". Like all the small dogs, Jack had a huge heart and would help anybody in trouble, but he didn't lack sense and self preservation had been instilled into him from puppyhood.

"I know, but I should've known there was no point. The cats lie, the Cairns twist things and the Bigs use those lies to win more power. I wasn't really brave, I was just so annoyed at what they did to poor Toby, I couldn't help myself." Elsie replied.

"Come come, Elsie, you were right to try to hold them to account," George joined in, his ginger whiskers bristling,"Do you think there will be recriminations for you speaking up?"

"I hope not. I think I didn't rile Sidney enough and I reckon Stu has a soft spot for me, he knew my mother you know, so he won't encourage retaliation. Ruby doesn't work that way, she will try to get me on her side to spread their lies and Titan obeys the others and doesn't really think for himself. The cats I try to avoid in any case, they sneak and lie and delight in torturing any poor creature they can. But, no, I'm not afraid they will actively seek me out for revenge, they will think they silenced my questions and thus the rest of the dogs." She smirked, "Perhaps I just need to be careful not to be seen with you small guys too much."

"Anyway," she continued, "I think they were right in that we need a plan. It does seem that a visit is due, just we don't really know the nature of it and they are trying to scare us for some reason. We will do well to be prepared."

"What do you think we can do?" asked Maisie. "We are so small and they are so big and hold all the power." She looked mournfully at her companions, "I don't see what I can do to stop them, they push me around as if they don't see me."

"That's true, but it also means that they don't notice smaller dogs as much and they don't see us as a threat to their control. We can go undetected and hide in small places and listen. We can find out information and use this to support each other to work against them. A sort of underground movement if you like." Elsie's eyes lit up as she spoke and the other dogs slowly started to nod in agreement.

"So, what you are saying is that we join together as a resistance fighting force?" Even Norris, who rarely thought of much except his stomach and playing tricks, was enthused now, "We fight back?"

"A bit less of the fighting if you please, not as obvious as that, but active, coordinated information gathering and resistance, yes."

"But where do we start, Elsie?" A small glimmer of hope showing in her face, Maisie was still doubtful.

"We get organised first. This place is great for meeting, so I suggest we make this our Headquarters and meet here nightly after tea, once everyone else is sleeping off their meals. They shouldn't miss us but we'll have to be wary of being spotted. We can always use an excuse. Perhaps you, Maisie, could start to put it about that you are feeling a little unwell?"

"I see what you mean Elsie, we need to fight back, but in our own way. We can use our talents to work together and against the system, to make things better." Jack too was impressed. "Does everyone agree, we'll work out how to do this thing?" As he looked round his friends, they all nodded back. "Okay, then let us plan!"

The small dogs talked quietly into the night as they slowly formulated a plan. Elsie, practical and determined as usual, suggested they join forces to listen and gather information and report back nightly to Headquarters or "HQ". Maisie offered to try to glean information from Max as he was a known informer but loved to talk about himself. She would also drop into conversation hints about her "illness". George suggested that the group could gather and share useful things such as emergency food supplies, so it was agreed he would be in charge of resources and the other dogs would let him know about anything that could be useful. Jack and Norris would work together, Norris to distract attention and Jack to slip quietly away to carry out resistance activities.

The first of those activities, it was agreed, was to support Toby in his solitary confinement. Elsie was still angry about his treatment. "How could they be so cruel?" she asked. " The Bigs were making a point, of course, to scare the other dogs into submission, and it worked! But we can help him, we must make sure he has supplies and at least some moral support. Think of it as our first operation!"

"That's right, let's help Toby," nodded Jack. "But how? They'll have frogmarched him off to solitary in the garage by now, and the Cairns will be guarding the door, there's no way of reaching him." The dogs slowly shook their heads as they tried to think of a way to help him.

Maisie, a thoughtful look in her eye, whispered, "I wonder…" and turned round to look at the wall at the back of the den.

"What is it, Maisie? What are you thinking?" Jack stared hard at where she was looking but saw nothing but old paint pots and brushes and rollers.

"Well, it's just that… Jack, do you remember the mice last winter?"

Jack nodded, he remembered fondly chasing the small, squeaky creatures but never being able to catch one. The mouse family had temporarily come into the house during the cold weather, looking for shelter and food. He'd heard their scratching noises above his head when he'd been trying to sleep in the den under the stairs and sometimes watched them scurry across the floor. But they were too quick for him and he'd had to content himself with a pounce and a chase that came to nothing. Still it was fun and when, in the spring, they'd moved out, he almost missed them.

"Well," said Maisie, more confidently now, "you see, I didn't chase them. In fact, I helped one escape once when a cat had it cornered. I distracted the cat and the mouse made a run for safety. Lizzie, I think it was, she was so cross with me but several dogs came along so she just spat at me and left. So, later that evening the mouse found me and thanked me. I could see she was frightened, she was quivering, but very bravely said thank you for rescuing me."

"That's just like you Maisie, always making friends, I just wanted to catch one of the cheeky little things."

She smiled. "Yes I know, they thought it funny too! The mouse told me that they liked to tease you because they knew you weren't fast enough to catch them. Anyway, we became friends and she told me her name was Minnie and that her family lived on the other side of the den wall, in the pantry next to the kitchen. She told me there was a hole between the pantry and the den, just behind those paint pots there and that from the pantry she could get out through a grill into the garage. Minnie invited me to visit, she reckoned I was small enough to slip through, but I was too frightened to try it. But I was thinking, maybe I could try now, for Toby's sake, you know?"

"It could work." Elsie had been listening closely and thought Maisie's idea might have some merit. "Why don't we clear out some of this stuff and take a look? George, you're closest, can you try moving some stuff out of the way?"

The dogs all turned around and George started to grab things and pass them to Norris who, together with Jack, piled them in the opposite corner of the crowded den. Brushes, rags and rollers were moved until, finally, just a heavy paint pot stood against the wall. Norris took hold of the handle and started to pull and George pushed his nose behind it to lever it out of the corner. Groaning and grunting, they worked together and finally shifted it. Behind where it had stood, was a small hole in the wall, just big enough for a very, very small dog to pass through.

"Minnie was right!" Maisies eyes were large in the dark. "It must go through to the pantry! Can, er... somebody try it?"

Sensing her nerves about the dark unknown space beyond, George stood up. "I'll go first, I can let you know what I find," he said, turning around and starting to put his head through the gap. He wriggled and turned his head from side to side, but after a few moments it was obvious he was getting nowhere. "No use," he declared, pulling back, "I'm too big! Someone smaller must try."

The dogs turned to look at Jack, who wasn't feeling very brave either. But he put on a brave face saying, "Move over then, I need some room." The dogs shuffled round, allowing Jack to take his place at the gap. He cautiously put his head into the hole and pushed his shoulders forward. After a short scramble his whole body disappeared through the hole until the dogs could only see his black splodged bottom and white tail receding further into the gloom. The dogs heard further scrambling, then it went quiet.

"Are you okay Jack?" Maisie was worried. The dogs listened but no sound came from the other side of the wall. "Jack, Jack, respond," she called. She waited a while, but no sound came. "It's no use, he can't hear me, stand aside, I'm going after him," she said bravely and squeezed her tiny body through the hole in the wall, just as he had. The dogs watched as her cream bottom and tail disappeared into the dark and, like Jack, she scrambled through and then all went quiet.

The dogs looked at each other. "We must wait," said Elsie, practically. "They must be beyond our hearing so we'll let them get on with it. Let's take it in turns to monitor the gap and stand ready to provide help, but we should rest now. George, you're on first watch."

George nodded and sat with his eyes on the gap, one ear tuned to any sounds that might come from beyond. Elsie and

Norris lay down and tried to snooze, but kept looking over towards the corner.

Chapter Six

Jack lay in the dark. He had scrambled through a sort of tunnel until he came out of the other side. He'd pushed his front paws through the gap and put them down, but on what? He sniffed. It smelt like cat litter and certainly felt like it. He put his paws down on the crunchy crumbling stuff and realised that he had, indeed, landed in an opened bag of cat litter. *Uggh!* He shuddered and hastily pulled his back paws through the gap and stepped forward and down onto the cool, tiled floor of the pantry.

It was very dark in the pantry, with just a glimmer of reflected light coming in through a grill on the wall to his left and under the door in front of him. It was also very quiet, he couldn't hear any of the sounds of his friends back in the den. Slowly he turned around, trying to identify the shapes surrounding him. He could just make out some more bags piled on the floor, sacks really and a quick sniff told him they were full of dried dog food and biscuits and at least one with cat crunchies in it. To the side were shelves with bottles and cans and small boxes with pouches of something on them which he thought he recognised, *cat food or meaty chunks, perhaps?*

A sound behind him made him start as a head, paws then body slithered through the gap and then fell forward through the cat litter and onto the floor. Maisie had arrived!

She picked herself up and, as he had done, she took a look around the pantry. "Wow, Jack! Look at all the food, we could feast like kings and queens!" She went towards the nearest bag of dog food, put her tiny nose in the top of the bag and breathed in.

"Yes," agreed Jack, watching her. "But I think we should be careful. We don't want anyone to know we've been here, if we leave no trace then we can return." He walked over to where a faint amber light shone through a grill on the wall, "I think this is the grill your mouse friend mentioned, it must lead to the garage." He pushed at the grill with his nose. The grill was made of plastic and was attached to the outside wall. As he pushed, the grill flipped outward and he could see into the garage. "See, Maisie, it *is* the garage out there," he told her, "could you come and hold the grill open for me so I can take a better look?"

Maisie came up alongside Jack and used her nose and a paw to push the grill forward. It seemed to be hinged from above, but could be pushed out far enough to allow a tiny dog to get through. The amber light seemed to be coming in from small windows set in the garage doors and it illuminated just enough of the garage so they could pick out shapes in the gloom. They could see boxes and heaps of rubbish piled high and over on the far wall stood an ancient rabbit hutch. They both knew that this was the prison Toby would be in. "There it is, Jack, that's where they'll have put poor Toby. How do we get there?"

Jack looked down. Immediately in front of the grill was a tray which seemed to contain old bits of wood and pine cones. "It's not too far to jump down, Maisie, but if I go then I think you'd best stay up here so you can hold the grill open for me. I'm going to check Toby's alright then I'll report back to you. We'll have to go quietly though, I don't want any of the Cairns to hear me, they'll be guarding the door back into the kitchen." As Maisie silently and solemnly nodded her agreement in the gloom, he nipped her playfully. "Cheer up, Maisie, it's an adventure!" he said and, as he saw her break into a slow smile, pushed his body forward and jumped out through the grill and down into the garage.

He landed on the pine cones. As he jumped off them and onto the garage floor, they released a faint smell of pine. *Good!* he thought. Be*tter they smell of pine - it'll put any cats off going too close to the grill to investigate!* He crossed the garage floor, carefully skirting around boxes and piles of rubbish, weaving his way until he stood silently in front of the rabbit hutch.

The hutch was an ancient wooden one that sat up high on tall legs. It had a wire front and a nest box to one side. The wired front was secured with a simple catch which could only be opened from outside. It hadn't seen a rabbit for years of course, but there was still a sprinkle of wood shavings on the floor and a few strands of musty hay inside. A small table was set in front of the hutch and this allowed access to it. Jack just needed to get up to the small table, but as a teeny, tiny dog, this was no mean feat. He looked around and saw a small box just under the hutch, *that would do*. He pulled and pushed and prodded the box until it was positioned just beside the table and thus acted as a step for him to climb on. He jumped up onto the box, then onto the table and stopped suddenly as he came face to face with a trembling Toby.

Toby was lying in the middle of the cage floor with his golden Spaniel ears flopped down over his eyes and his paws over them. On his nose he still bore a bright slash from his cruel cat punishment earlier and he was shaking from head to toe with fear. Jack hissed quietly through the wire door, "Toby, it's me, Jack! Don't be frightened, I've come to help you."

Toby couldn't hear him and continued to quiver, so Jack looked up and around, inspecting the cage door until his eyes alighted on the catch. He nudged it with his nose until it swivelled around and the cage door was free. Taking hold of the corner of the door with his teeth, he pulled it a little way open until he could slip through the gap and into the cage. He touched Toby's paw with his nose, but Toby simply shook harder and made a small whimpering sound. Jack pulled gently at Toby's paw and whispered harder into his ear, "Toby! It's Jack, open your eyes!"

This seemed to do the trick and Toby slowly took one paw away from his ear, pushed his ear back and opened one eye to look. Jack sat back so the glimmer of light from the streetlamp outside shone on him, reflecting orange off his white fur, "Toby! I've come to help you."

"Jack?" Toby mouthed. "Jack, is it really you?" he whispered as he removed his paw from his other ear and now looked at Jack with both eyes. "Jack it is you! I thought you were a m...m...monster!"

Jack knew how frightened Toby was to be on his own and also guessed rightly that the Cairns would have fed into that fear before enacting his punishment. "No monsters here, Toby," he grinned, "just me come to help you. Come, sit up and let me look at you." He started to check Toby over, investigating carefully with his nose. Besides trembling a little still and ignoring the wound on his nose, Toby seemed to be in one piece, but he sat up and let his tiny friend sniff him all over and soothe his fears.

When the check was over, Toby finally asked, "But how come you're here, Jack, how did you get past the Cairns and especially the m...monsters?"

Jack smiled grimly, they'd really done a job on his friend, *How dare they frighten him so much with talk of monsters?* But he kept that thought to himself and patiently explained how the small dogs had started to organise themselves and that Elsie had suggested the first mission was to support Toby. He told him how he and Maisie had slipped into the pantry with all its food delights and then how he had dropped into the garage and found him in his prison. "But that way is only for tiny dogs, Toby, you are too big to fit through any of the gaps. In any case, we need you to stay here, we don't want to raise suspicions."

Toby's eyes had lit up at two of the things Jack had mentioned, the first was Elsie. "Elsie stood up for me, you know. She helped me when they hurt me in the dog council, despite the risks of being seen to help me and she's helping me now by sending you. I owe her a lot, she's a good friend." The second thing that elicited a response was Jack's mention of food, "You know Jack, I'm starving. I only had the cat crunchies for breakfast that you gave me and then I was too nervous before the dog council to eat much. You mentioned food in the pantry?"

"Yes there's food there, if we're careful I think we can get you some. Come with me over to the grill, we can ask Maisie to help." Jack turned around and pushed at the cage door until it swung more widely open, "Follow me." Both dogs stepped through the cage opening and onto the table in front, then Jack jumped onto the box below and then the floor, Toby simply jumped all the way down. They wove their way between the rubbish and the boxes over to the grill on the wall. "Maisie, are you there?" hissed Jack, "I've brought Toby over and he needs food."

The grill lifted slightly and Maisie's cream head peaked out, "Hi Toby, I thought you'd be hungry, would a pouch of cat food work for you? You'd need to tear it open yourself, because my teeth aren't big enough."

"Yes please, Maisie! Don't worry, I can open it, just pass it down here."

"Wait a minute then," Maisie's head disappeared for a minute or two. When she came back she had a pouch in her mouth which she pushed out under the grill and watched it fall into the pine cones below.

Toby stepped forward and picked the pouch out of the pine cones. He held it down on the floor with one paw and ripped the end of the pouch off with his teeth. "Thanks," he mumbled as he started gulping the cat food down hungrily. He slurped and chewed until all the cat food was gone and sat looking at the empty packet.

"We'd better hide that in the rubbish," said Jack. "We don't want anyone to suspect we've been here." He picked up the scraps of the plastic pouch and put them under one of the rubbish piles nearby.

Meanwhile, Maisie had disappeared back into the pantry and returned with some dog biscuits in her mouth. "Here boys, we have biscuits to enjoy too!" She passed some down, then all three dogs sat and ate them in companionable silence.

Finally the last crumb was eaten and Toby sat back, "Thanks you guys, I don't know what I'd have done without you. I was so scared of the monsters, the Cairns told me they'd come and get me if I made any noise." He looked sheepish, "I guess they were lying to keep me quiet and to punish me."

Maisie was looking at the vivid red scratch that still showed on his nose. "That scratch looks painful, Toby. They're just cruel, those Cairns and the Bigs and, yes the cats too - because they do their dirty work. What right have they got to punish you for chasing Postie?" she said angrily. "As for frightening you witless about monsters too, well, it's as if they don't want us to go outside in case we find something out. They're using you as an example to frighten the rest of us I suppose. Why can that be, I wonder?"

"Indeed," agreed Jack. "They're up to something, they don't want us to go outside or to speak to anyone else. I don't suppose the story they're telling us about the visitors is entirely truthful, but how do we find out?" He looked pensive, "Toby, you know I told you how the small dogs are getting organised? Well, we'll need friends, friends who can find things out and tell us. Will you be one of those for our group?"

"Gladly! Anything you guys need, I'll help. But right now I'm thirsty after those biscuits, I thought I could smell some water somewhere?" Toby got up and went sniffing around the garage until he found a small bowl over by the door to the kitchen with some water in it. This he thirstily lapped up, "I think it's for the cats." He grinned, "Well, it's mine now."

After another quick sniff around the floor, he came back to where Jack and Maisie were, one sat up higher, watching out from the grill, the other sitting patiently below. "So, what's the plan now? How do we beat those brutes?"

The two small friends exchanged a smile, relieved to see Toby more upbeat and back to his normal self. For now, they agreed, it was important that their little group was careful not to be found out. They would come back and support Toby in his solitary confinement each night, but they must be careful and hide all evidence of their visit. Toby must go back in the cage at daybreak and Jack would close the latch and stow away his step so the Cairns would not know he'd been there. Toby would act chastened in the morning, glad to be let out of his prison after the long, scary night.

This being agreed, the dogs settled down to a night of chatting and telling stories, with Toby and Jack gently scratching and nipping each other and then settling down to snooze as the night wore on. Finally, the glimmering dawn penetrated the darkness through the windows of the garage and Maisie suggested it was time for her and Jack to leave. Toby nodded his golden head and walked across the floor to the hutch cage, jumped up and went inside. He turned to face Jack as his friend jumped up behind him and closed and latched the door, "Thank you, Jack, thank all the small dogs for me." He lay down, with his legs curled under his body, as Jack nodded to him then turned to leave.

The small dog jumped down to the floor, carefully stowing his box under the table, before making his way back across to the grill and, with a quick scramble, he was gone.

Once back inside the pantry Jack looked at Maisie, "I think we should be getting back to the others now. We could take them some more of the food, they'd like that.

Maisie shook her head, "I think we should be careful Jack, we don't want to raise suspicions. Anyway we can always come back if we need to, but I think it would be best if we took things just a very little at a time."

"Sensible as always Maisie, you're right of course, let's just go back then. After you." He turned to let her go past him and watched her jump up onto the bag of cat litter and scramble through the hole in the wall. She disappeared into the hole in the wall and he followed, huffing a little as he squeezed his shoulders through the gap.

On the other side, the other small dogs were waiting, having been roused from sleep by the sound of Maisie scrambling through. Much sniffing and wagging of tails later, they settled down to tell the story of their night's work and how they'd helped Toby.

"So there's food in there?" queried Elsie. "Well, well, well, that could be useful. You did the right thing not taking too much, we don't want anyone getting suspicious. But Toby needed it so that was alright. George, you're in charge of resources, what do you think we should do about the food?"

George had a thoughtful look on his face, "I think it's best left where it is for now. We have two dogs who can reach it if need be and it's probably in the safest place, because the other dogs and cats can't get to it. Yes, we'll leave it be, just use it when we have real need, like Jack did last night for Toby." The other small dogs nodded their agreement.

Elsie stood up, "It's starting to get light, so I think we'd better split up and leave the den now before anyone else stirs. Maisie don't forget now, you're to act ill and everyone else are to find out what they can and report back here tonight."

One by one the small dogs peeked out of the den and, seeing it was safe, quietly slipped out into the hall.

Chapter Seven

Wednesday dawned slowly in the dog house. The light filtered in via gaps in the ragged curtains and shone through broken glass panes, and steadily it became brighter in the house. The animals snoozed, stretched and scratched, then snoozed again. Minor squabbles occasionally broke out and were resolved with a snap or a grunt, but mainly the house was quiet and peaceful. Until the human got up.

The dogs heard the human get out of bed, putting old, weary feet into old, weary slippers and slowly padding across to the bathroom. This was the signal for activity to start. In the kitchen the Cairns, who had avoided a lockdown of their own by the human, had been taking it in turns to do sentry duty. Now they nudged the door to the garage open, marched down the steps, crossed the cool, concrete floor and released the latch holding Toby prisoner in the hutch. "Come on Toby, make it snappy!" barked Stu. "Time to be going, you be quick about it!"

Toby, relieved they hadn't noticed anything different, needed no more persuasion and jumped down out of the hutch and bounded across the garage floor and into the house, followed swiftly by the Cairns.

In the house the animals were starting to move, the dogs who had not been shut away were milling around the floor in the hall and kitchen. The cats slunk down the stairs, sidled into the kitchen and jumped up onto the work surfaces, swiping spitefully at any dog noses that got in their way. "Sssss," hissed Lizzie, her fluffy tail twitching haughtily as she passed through the dogs. "Watch out, dogssss, make way for catssss!" she lisped. The cats were fed first and they fussily picked their way through the cat food and scattered cat crunchies across the worktop until they had eaten their fill. Then, as if they shared a silent signal, they turned and slipped out of the kitchen.

Once more it was meaty chunks morning and the same mayhem and unfair system of feeding ensued. The small dogs met up in the kitchen den in good time and gave a nod to Toby out in the main kitchen, who created a small distraction by arguing with Max over a dish of food. The small dogs pulled in two plates of food this time and hid them under the units. They ate their way through one plate full and, when the bigger dogs had left the room, pushed the other back out and shared it with Toby, Elsie and a hungry looking Yorkshire Terrier who thanked them profusely.

The small dogs made sure Maisie breakfasted well, a necessary part of the deceit that was to come, and she drank her fill at the water bowl. She was watched over by Jack, "There's a good girl, Maisie, now play your part and see what you can find out. I'm sure you can smooth talk Max if you try, he loves to impress."

"Yes," added George, drily, "Max just loves to impress a lady." He gently nudged her side, and whispered gruffly, "Take care, Maisie, watch out for the cats, they sneak around you know."

"I'll be fine, George, I'll keep my eyes open and I know I've got backup with you guys." Maisie spoke softly, then she turned and walked calmly out of the kitchen, crossed the hall and went over to the living room.

At the door she stopped to look around the room. Various bigger dogs were sleeping on the floor and the furniture and a couple of dogs were having a small tussle over a piece of rag in the corner. Maisie spied her quarry. Max was lying stretched out on the comfy chair, long sleek black body stretched out, ears drooping and tongue lolling as he slept. She crossed the room and sat down in front of him.

"Hello Max, how are you?" she asked in a lowered voice, remembering her instructions to act unwell and keeping her eyes and ears down to match.

"Why hello! Maisie isn't it? I'm fine, couldn't be better, nice breakfast and now a pretty lady has popped by to see me. At your service Ma'am, what can I do for you?" Max stretched out his glossy limbs, and shook his curly head.

My, aren't you just the handsome one? Maisie wasn't fooled, she knew that beneath that handsome face and strong body, Max thought only of himself and very little for others. He had charm though, she acknowledged and smiled to herself, *this may be fun!*

Max saw the smile, "Social call hey? Can't say I blame you, jump up here with me and we'll continue our cosy chat. I've been wanting to get to know you better."

His eyes fixed intently on her and she suppressed a shudder. Thinking quickly, she remembered her act and started to employ her story. "No er… but thanks, Max. I can't really, you see… I'm not feeling very well and that's a big jump for someone like me. I'm feeling quite woozy. In fact… I think I'd better stay on the floor."

Max narrowed his eyes and stared at her, "As you wish. Why are you feeling woozy? Have you had breakfast?"

"I er… it was busy again…" Maisie let her voice trail off and allowed the words to hang in the air. She knew Max couldn't resist an opportunity to tell her what she'd done wrong and to tell her how he'd have done better.

"You missed it again, didn't you? No wonder you're feeling ill. You should have done what I said yesterday when I tipped you off. I don't know why I waste my time with you! Did you even make an attempt this morning?"

Maisie hung her head and kept her eyes focused on the floor. Better he didn't see that dangerous glint that was forming, "I'm sorry Max, it's just... All the bigger dogs scare me, they push me around."

"Rubbish, you just don't try hard enough, that's all, you're weak. You've only got yourself to blame if you're feeling ill now." He paused, recollecting himself and finally looking at her. "Don't cry, Maisie, it doesn't matter now. Hey, don't spoil those pretty girl looks." He looked at her, his head on one side and handsome face breaking into a smile. "Give me a smile now and let's forget it."

Maisie, internally comparing the very different responses to her distress at not getting a share of meaty chunks, couldn't help but smile. This smile, though, was at the thought of a small and gruff ginger dog with white paws, the one who'd saved AND fed her. Max was all words and no action she realised but, playing the game some more, she smiled at him.

"That's better! Now I'll tell you a story, did you hear about Toby last night?" Max continued, cluelessly.

"N... no," she replied, hesitantly. Maisie didn't want to give anything away.

She needn't have worried. Max loved to talk, mostly about himself, but often in ways that showed others in a poor light. "Oh yes, Toby, what a state! Well, after they'd finished with him at dog council, they kept a close eye on him, y'know, so he couldn't hide but had to serve his punishment. When it was nearly lockdown time, they summoned him to the kitchen. Then, ha ha ha, his knees were actually knocking together, he was shaking so hard!"

Max laughed as he recalled the story, finding Toby's distress amusing, "well, the Cairns were there with their serious faces on and they said they were going to lock him up in that old rabbit hutch in the garage for the night then leave him there on his own.

Sue reiterated it was punishment for going outside and breaking the rule, which was only there for his and all the rest of the dogs' safety. So, at this point, he asks if that's because of the monsters and Sue tells him yes it is!" Max was enjoying his story immensely, "Toby's standing there, about to go into solitary in the garage and he looks at me. Well, I just couldn't help myself, I... I warned him to be careful out there, because the monsters sometimes came to the garage!" Max gave in to a series of belly rumbling laughs as he remembered his trick. "You know what Maisie? He actually peed himself with fright there and then in the kitchen! Stu had to bite his leg to get him to move and I could still hear him whimpering as they led him away..." He wiped his eyes, the joke was a good one.

Maisie stood with her eyes still down so he couldn't see the anger in them, *how very, very, cruel!* Now she understood Toby's terror better and she was so glad the small dogs had organised a support mission. Of course, she kept this to herself, she had information to get. Steeling herself to keep her voice level, she thought she'd try to catch him out, "Max, that wasn't a nice trick to play, especially when you know there aren't any monsters really."

"Oh I know, but it was so funny!" Max fell for her ruse, so keen was he to share his joke. "Maisie, he actually peed on the floor as they led him away!"

Sensing a chance to get some truth, Maisie smiled too, "Peed indeed, he must have believed you! But why monsters Max?"

"Oh, that! It was something Sidney made up." Max scratched an ear and admired his own paw. "Sidney said we needed something to frighten the dogs and stop them disobeying the rules, so he suggested monsters. It was quite easy to put the story around, the cats just had to have a few supposed close encounters and everyone believed it. It's just so funny how Toby was taken in so totally by it though! That'll serve him right for going outside, he'll think twice when he sees Postie again!"

"It was a good joke," Maisie agreed. "You're right, it'll keep him from Postie," she added, taking a guess that this was important somehow.

Still chuckling to himself, Max continued, "Stupid Toby! But yeah, don't want him talking to Postie, he might find something out he shouldn't."

Careful. Now that she had him talking, she didn't want him to clam up. "What could Postie possibly know that would be of interest to Toby?"

"Postie brings the letters you see. He brought the one last week to the human, the cats read it."

"Oh?" Nonchalantly now, she examined her claws. "The letter?"

"The letter about the visitors. The human put it on the dining table and the cats read it up there. That's how they found out, but Sidney didn't want the news to get out until they were ready."

"News?" She had him talking now.

"Oh you know, news and stuff, the usual." His tone had changed. No longer laughingly conspiratorial, he brushed off her question and she looked up quickly at him, questioning. "You really should eat something, Maisie, you'll feel better if you do." Max rolled over and sat up and she became aware of a large shape behind her. "Oh hello, Titan. Maisie missed out on breakfast this morning, she's not feeling too well."

Titan ignored Maisie. "Sidney wants a word," he grunted. "Now!"

"Ok, I'm coming," Max stood up and shook his fine body then jumped down from the chair. "They can't run the place without me," he whispered in Maisie's ear as he followed Titan out of the room.

Maisie watched him leave. He was something to behold, all glossy, black fur and strong, muscled body. But Max was a fraud, a self-serving fake who'd played a dirty trick on her friend and who was part of some bigger game that would, she reckoned, harm them all. She needed to report back, she decided, and headed for hall HQ.

At the living room door she bumped into Norris who was playing tag with another dog. "Everything OK, Maisie?" She nodded and he resumed his game. Maisie wasn't fooled, even if it looked like an innocent greeting to others, she knew he'd been keeping an eye out for her. It felt good to have friends.

One by one, within the next hour, the small dogs assembled at HQ. They did so slowly and carefully to avoid being seen, but finally they were all sitting in the den, eyes on Maisie.

Maisie's first mission had gone well and she passed on what Max had told her. She noted how Elsie's eyes narrowed as she mentioned Max's obvious and callous amusement at Toby's distress. She saw George's quick look of concern for her when she told them about Max's engaging but lying ways but she quickly reassured her friends that she'd not been fooled by Max, instead had just played along. She repeated what he'd said about the monsters' story being a way to control the dogs and a reason not to let them go outside where they might find things out. Finally, she told them about the cats reading the letter containing news about the visitors and how the Bigs didn't want the news to get out just yet. "I don't know what it means but we're all being lied to for some reason, I'm sorry I didn't find out more."

"You did really well, Maisie, you kept Max talking for long enough that he told you useful things and hopefully didn't suspect you." Elsie was full of praise, she knew the little Chihuahua had been frightened but had approached the mission with a brave heart. "It's clear there's something going on that they dont want us to know the truth about, so we're just going to have to do some more digging."

The small dogs agreed and nudged and patted Maisie for her brave work. They then settled down to discuss the next stage of the plan. "It would be useful if we could see the letter," stated Elsie. "Can anyone here read human words?"

Jack shyly raised a paw. "I can recognise some of the letters. My mother taught me when I was a puppy."

"Right, then, we need a ruse to get you onto the dining room table and a distraction whilst you look for the letter." Elsie looked at Norris and George. "I've got a plan, but I'll need your help."

Elsie quickly outlined the plan, Maisie was to have no part in it, her work getting information was too valuable to risk her being caught. Besides, it was time for her to rest. Elsie herself would supervise the letter operation from a little way away but the boys would carry out the mission between them. She told them all their parts and made a final check they understood what they were to do.

Chapter Eight

The small dogs surreptitiously left HQ and split up, each intent on their part of the plan. Elsie wove her way through dogs in the living room until she found Toby who was sitting on the carpet scratching his flea bites. She whispered in his ear until he nodded his understanding then he followed her to the dining room where, with a few deft nudges, furniture pieces were repositioned. Jack went to the kitchen and into the den under the units where he found his old friend, the chewed up sock. He picked it up in his mouth, gave it one last appreciative chew, and crept carefully out of the den, taking care not to be noticed.

He walked over to the dining room doorway where Norris and George had taken up positions. He broke into a trot as he passed his cousin. "Hey Norris, look what I've got!" The two small dogs started to chase and tussle over the sock and fell laughing into the dining room.

Feeling the disapproving stares of the other dogs on them as they fought, and knowing there would probably be retribution for 'playing with a toy', Jack and Norris played with the sock, tugging and leaping together. Somehow, it wasn't quite clear how it happened, the sock became airborne and it flew up and landed on the dining room table. Jack immediately followed and stepped up a neatly positioned step stool, onto a dining chair and thus onto the table where he found his sock.

Just at this moment, however, everyone's attention was drawn to a commotion in the doorway. George, it seemed, had taken exception to Toby bounding past him exuberantly and knocking the smaller dog slightly. "Careful!" he growled. "Watch your step, young 'un, have some respect."

Toby had slithered to a halt and was apologising, "I'm sorry George, I didn't think...."

Uncharacteristically grumpy now, the small dog continued as everyone turned to watch him tear a strip off the unfortunate Toby. "That's just it, Toby! You never think of others and the effect your actions might have on them. Why, you even went outside the other day!" He took a quick look around, subtly checking he had everyone's attention, then continued to grumble loudly, "I'll bet you didn't think then how much you put us smaller dogs at risk with your careless behaviour!"

Jack and his toy forgotten, the dogs watched, amazed as George, usually gruff and a dog of few words, really started in on Toby. Toby apologised again yet George repeated various grumpy allegations around Toby's lack of sense, his carelessness and thoughtlessness towards others. Out of the corner of his eye George saw Jack quickly scan the table top, grab something, hiding it behind the sock which he'd also picked up, and then skip back down the way he had climbed up. He caught a nod from Elsie and he started to move further into the dining room, still grumbling at Toby whilst Jack passed something to Norris, who quietly slipped out the doorway and made his way to hall HQ to drop off a small item.

George, his job done, now looked at Toby. "Well I suppose it can't be helped now, you are young and silly after all. Just try to be more careful in future." He walked sulkily off, leaving a relieved Toby staring after him, slightly confused as to whether he had really earned all the words of disapprobation dealt to him or if George had simply enjoyed embellishing his act somewhat.

A few hours later, having played, groomed, snoozed, eaten some dog crunchies and lapped at some water, the small dogs reconvened at HQ. During the afternoon the weather outside had worsened and even in their den the dogs could hear the wind howling around and the rain lashing on the windows of the house.

They knew it would sound even worse in the garage so the first decision was to agree to support Toby in solitary confinement once more. Meanwhile, they had an interesting item to study.

Norris tugged the item out of the old sock which he'd stashed in the corner. It was a piece of paper with typewritten words on it and an official looking letterhead. He turned to look at Jack, "Well Jack, can you read it? What does it say?"

Jack smoothed the paper out with his paws, close to the entrance of the den so that light from the hall was cast upon it. "Let's see... I think these words at the top are addresses, who it's to and from and stuff. Yes, those characters are numbers - '2' and then '5'. That's our house number, twenty five, so that part must be our address. The other one I can't quite make out, but I think that word is 'council'. That makes sense, it's a letter to our human from the council."

Elsie was listening intently, "Council, Jack? Is that a human council then? I hope it's not like our dog council. That would be bad news, I'm not surprised the Bigs are worried!"

"I don't know, let's see if I can read some more," Jack squinted hard at the letter. "I think that word there is the humans' name, so they know who they're writing to then. The other words are hard ones, there's one beginning with a w letter and one that I think is check. A w... check and then another number, '3' I think and... that one I recognise, it's 'Friday'."

"A w... check on Friday 3rd, Jack, is that what it says?"

"I think so, a w...e...l... something check." Jack scrunched his eyes up but the letters didn't make any more sense to him.

Elsie tried to make sense of it. "Wel... welcome, wellbeing, wellness, welfare? Oh! It could be any of those I suppose, it doesn't really matter. It looks like the council is going to do a wel...fare check on Friday 3rd."

"That's the day after tomorrow," Maisie spoke softly and they turned to look at her.

"How do you know that, Maisie?" asked Elsie.

"I saw the human turn the thing called a calendar over today. I like to watch it because it has a new picture when they do that, today it was beautiful pink flowers in a pretty garden. Anyway, when they do that it is always on the 1st of the new month, so today must be Wednesday 1st and Friday 3rd is the day after tomorrow."

"Good point, Maisie, but that means we haven't got much time. Jack, can you work out when on Friday the visit will be?"

"Let me see," Jack scrunched his eyes up even harder in concentration, "I think that is it, those numbers there, '1' then '2' and then some more letters I don't understand, n-o-o-n."

"One, two, is that twelve Jack? And could that n-o word be noon?" Elsie was quick to work it out. "That would make sense, noon is midday, halfway between dawn and dusk." A door banged somewhere in the house and a draught gusted into the den, lifting the corner of the paper up. "Storm's getting up, better not leave Toby too long! But what about this letter, what does it all mean?"

"It makes sense to me," chipped in George. "They're coming at midday on Friday to check if the human is okay. Perhaps the human council heard how the Bigs run this place and they want to check it out for themselves. I'll bet the Bigs want the rest of us out of the way so they can control the visit and so the visitors don't suspect how they really manage the place."

"George has a point, it explains why they're being so secretive about the visit and why they're getting Sue and Stu to organise the place and hide the dogs. Oh yes and why the Bigs have nominated themselves as the reception committee." Elsie frowned in concentration, "I see it now. But do they really think they'll fool the visitors?"

"They could do," Maisie said softly. "They'll control the dogs with fear of being punished like poor Toby, so they'll do as told. That's what all this unfair punishment of him has been about - it's a show, put on to warn the rest of the dogs to follow their stupid rules." Bitterly now as the thoughts joined up in her head and tumbled out, she continued, "Yes, the Cairns will do the dirty work, they'll keep the other dogs locked up in the dining room, watching them like hawks so they make no noise. The cats will stay out of the way and the Bigs will shepherd the visitors into the living room and make sure the visit goes as planned. They've got it planned out well."

"So we'll need to work our own plan out then. What if we were to refuse to go into the dining room and make a fuss when the visitors arrive?" Elsie was thinking hard, "No, I don't think such direct tactics would work, the Bigs would simply push and pull us into the dining room and the Cairns would punish us if we moved or made a sound."

"They can't catch all of us at the same time, and what if we were hiding?" Norris had been following the conversation. "I'd be up for distracting the Bigs for a bit if someone else wants to welcome the visitors."

And so the small dogs batted around ideas for foiling the Bigs' plan. They mulled over and rejected various ideas which required superdog strength or heroics - after all they were all very small dogs, but finally they settled on a plan of their own.

On Thursday evening, before dog lockdown happened, they would all take their places in the various dens. This meant that they could stay hidden until the visit, ready to spring out and surprise the visitors. They would need supplies so they didn't have to join the breakfast queue where they would be captured and made to follow the Bigs' plan. George would work with Jack and Maisie to ensure every den had food and water for the night, Jack said he had an idea about the water. George and Maisie would be in the comfy chair den in the living room, Elsie and Norris in the kitchen den under the units and Jack would be in the hall HQ. All dogs were to remain quiet and hidden whilst the visitors were met and shown in. Once the visitors had concluded their visit, then the small dogs would appear and try to make them understand how the Bigs ran the place by jumping up and barking. Norris, who had the longest legs and loudest bark, would run up and shout the loudest to attract the visitors' attention and warn them.

Hopefully, the Bigs would be taken by surprise and would not be able to do much about it. Retribution would come later of course, were they still prepared to do it? Yes, they all solemnly nodded, it was worth it, and so the plan was agreed.

"Now," Elsie said, "We need to organise supplies." She cocked her head to one side, listening to the howling wind and spattering rain outside. "And we need to support Toby."

As on the previous night, firstly Jack and then Maisie squeezed their way through to the pantry. Whilst Jack slipped quietly through the grill into the garage, Maisie started to round up supplies of meaty chunks, cat food pouches, dog biscuits and cat crunchies. She was careful not to take them all from the same place so it would be less obvious that food had been removed, hopefully it wouldn't be noticed. She lined all the supplies up by the gap back to the den and hissed to George she was ready. The small dogs worked steadily through the night to pass the supplies out of the pantry and stack them in the main den.

Meanwhile, Jack worked his way across the floor towards the rabbit hutch. The storm was at its full height and could be heard more loudly in the garage. The wind whipped up the branches of a tree outside and they tap, tap, tapped on the window. Just like the previous time, Jack pushed the small box out to make a step and jumped up to the table in front of the hutch.

He could see by the amber glow of the street light outside the shivering shape of Toby in the hutch. As before, he undid the latch to the door and pushed it open. Just as he did this, an extra strong gust of wind outside brought the tree branches banging onto the garage roof and the shivering Toby let out a crying noise. Jack didn't bother to try to speak over the storm, he nudged his friend's shoulder with his nose, and softly breathed into his ear. Toby responded and lifted his head to look at him, "Jack, it is you! Oh Jack I've been so scared," he sniffed Jack's nose. "Thanks for coming to help me."

Again, Jack led the way out of the cage and jumped down to the floor, Toby following but flinching at the sounds of the storm. "Are you sure it's safe, Jack? Sounds awfully angry out there, are you certain it's not monsters?"

Jack smiled sympathetically at Toby's mention of monsters, he was pretty sure the Cairns would have taken advantage of the storm to further frighten Toby. And indeed they had, Toby told him how Sue had warned him to be quiet because of the storm. He also told him how Max had just happened to pass by again and helpfully mentioned that he shouldn't draw any attention on such a stormy night when monsters were known to prowl around under the cover of the sounds of the storm. This had upset and frightened Toby again and even though he had tried to be brave when the sounds of the storm were so loud, all he could think about were Max's words about monsters.

They were standing over by the grill by this time and Jack hissed Maisie's name. After a few moments her little nose appeared. "Hello Toby, are you hungry again?" When Toby nodded she added, "Well I'm quite busy tonight, sorting out supplies for 'Operation Visitors' on Friday, but I've got you a cat food pouch and some biscuits for you both. I'll pass them down to you and Jack can fill you in on what's going on whilst I do my work up here." Her nose briefly disappeared then returned and pushed out a cat food pouch and several biscuits.

So the dogs sat and ate the food and Jack updated Toby on what they'd found out that day, the contents of the letter, the welfare check on Friday and the small dogs' aim to foil the Bigs' plan. He told him why Maisie was busy getting supplies organised and then he paused, not quite knowing how to say the next bit. Finally, he told Toby how his cruel punishment had all been for show, a lesson for the other dogs, and that he'd been a victim of a wider conspiracy to keep the dogs uninformed and fearful of disobeying rules.

"Ah!" said Toby, the amber street light reflecting in his eyes. "That makes more sense now, I wondered why they singled me out and why they wanted to terrify me. I could have sworn I saw Max smirk at Sue when he told me about the storm covering the monster noises and he saw me shake and whimper as they led me into the garage." The expression on his face hardened, "You know Jack, I know I'm a bit bigger than you guys, so I can't fit in your dens and I know I do a lot of silly things like chase people and stuff, but if there is anything I can do to help you and to foil this plan of the Bigs, then count me in."

"You already helped this afternoon when you allowed George to pick a fight with you to distract the dogs' attention whilst I stole that letter," Jack reminded him. "But, as it happens, I do have another job you can help me with tonight. We need to collect some water for the supplies and I remembered seeing some empty plastic bottles in the rubbish piles. If we collect some small ones and try to fill them up, we can pass them up to Maisie."

Toby agreed to help and the two dogs went sniffing around the garage floor, checking the piles of rubbish for plastic bottles. They soon found what they were looking for and within a few moments had collected up a small pile of bottles, some with and some without caps.

Jack chewed thoughtfully on a cap, "If we can get the caps on and off we can fill them full. The others, we'll just have to half fill and try to keep them upright."

"But how will we fill them?" Toby wanted to know.

"Luckily it's a wet night, the storm has helped us out here, see over there, where there's a split in the roof panel? The rainwater is dripping down in several places. We just have to put a bottle under each drip and wait for it to fill up. Do you think you can do that?" Jack looked at Toby.

Toby nodded and together the dogs started to move the bottles, placing them carefully under the drips until they started to fill. Toby sat and watched the bottles, checking them from time to time during the night, moving them around until they were all filled to suitable levels. It took his mind away from the noise of the storm and he forgot to be frightened as he concentrated on each bottle and how it was filling up.

Jack meanwhile popped up through the grill to help Maisie with the food, returning just as it was starting to get light. "Toby, that's a fantastic job you've done there. Now we must get them passed up quickly before the day breaks and they come to get you." The dogs worked to pull and carry the bottles over to the grill and passed them carefully up to Maisie.

As the last bottle was passed up, Jack turned to Toby. "Back to the cage, Toby, but just for now."

As on the previous night Toby went back to the hutch, jumped up into it and then lay down curled up whilst Jack latched the cage front, jumped down and stowed away his box. "Thank you my friend, I won't forget your help." Jack nodded and scurried quickly away, checking the garage looked as it should, before he jumped up and wriggled through the grill once more.

Inside the pantry, Maisie had been busy and there were just two bottles of water left to pass through to HQ. Jack helped her to push them through, then did a last check before they both scrambled back, *nobody should suspect a thing,* he thought.

Back in HQ, the walls seemed to have moved closer in. Food and water supplies were stacked in every corner and it was a tight squeeze for all the small dogs to fit. George had done a wonderful job of organising the supplies as Maisie had passed them up and he spent the next few minutes explaining to everyone how they were to be distributed, so that everyone would be stocked up in their respective hiding places.

"How was Toby, Jack?" asked Elsie, concern showing in her soft brown eyes. Jack told her how the Cairns had bullied him once more and how Max had taken further delight in scaring him about the storm. He described how he'd found him whimpering and shaking with fright, then he told her how he'd set him to work on the water bottles task which had absorbed his interest and helped him forget his fears.

Elsie fumed, "Those evil dogs, they don't care who they hurt as long as they keep their system working!" Then her expression softened. "But I'm so glad we could support him, that spoiled their fun a little." Firmer now, she said, "We must make our little plan work, we have to break their hold on this place."

Chapter Nine

As Thursday dawned a familiar routine broke out in the household. Once the human could be heard getting out of bed upstairs, the small dogs started to leave HQ so that by breakfast time they all appeared from different parts of the house. Toby was released from his prison by the Cairns and the cats strutted silently down the stairs, swiping at any stray nose or paw that got in their way. Breakfast time was uneventful as it was dry dog food this morning and there was plenty for all to share. It distracted the hungry animals of the house who didn't notice as the small dogs quietly left and moved their supplies from HQ and secreted them inside the other dens.

There was a bustle about the house this morning, though, as the Bigs and the Cairns started to put their plan into action. The human seemed to have caught onto it too as, in a rare display of industry, the house was tidied and cleaned. This resulted in the living room and hall, at least, becoming less cluttered and evidence of dog soiling was washed and scrubbed away. Piles of mess and rubbish items were bagged up together and moved to join the piles of rubbish in the garage. It didn't completely remove all traces, of course, but the place slowly transformed and began to look and smell a little more presentable.

The tidying and cleaning took most of the day, with the Cairns barking orders at the other dogs, who milled around and moved things, only to find they'd got it wrong and had to move them back again. The cats swiftly surveyed the mayhem and disappeared outside, only to reappear at tea time once the job was done. The Bigs took up residence on the big green sofa in the living room so they could watch the work but not actively be involved, and their brooding presence served to worry and fluster the other dogs who made more mistakes. Max took it upon himself to wander around the work parties, making sure they got a good view of his grand physique and strong, good looks, before reporting progress back to the Bigs. Sue and Stu meanwhile growled and nipped at any dog who slacked in their work or made a mistake.

One such dog was Maisie. Conscious of Max and the tale she'd told him the day before, and still anxious to get whatever information she could, she continued to feign illness and worked more slowly than the others. This, of course, brought her under the scrutiny of Sue who was harrying the smaller dogs to get them to pull items of rubbish out from under furniture so they could be removed from the house. Sue nipped her on the shoulder. "You must work faster, nobody can be lazy today."

Maisie jumped but said nothing as Max had just arrived to conduct his survey of the work party.

"Faster," hissed Sue in her ear, aware that Max was approaching them and not entirely immune to his charms herself.

"Morning ladies, and what do we have here?" Max smiled at them both.

His smile doesn't reach his eyes, thought Maisie, but stayed silent.

"This dog here is lazy and not working fast enough," barked Sue, standing upright to give her report.

"Is this so, Maisie? I thought we'd discussed how important it was that we all prepare for the visit?" Max looked enquiringly at her.

"I'm still not feeling very well, I didn't get any breakfast today either." Maisie played her part well, her eyes downcast and tail drooping between her hind legs.

"That's true, I didn't see you at breakfast, " admitted Max. "I told you how you should do it though, Maisie. I really don't see why you make it so hard for yourself."

Maisie was aware of another pair of eyes unobtrusively watching this interaction. George, his ginger moustache bristling at every one of Max's words, knew the part she was playing yet was frustrated at being unable to intervene. She spoke feebly, "Yes I know Max, but I'm feeling rather faint just now…" She wobbled then sank to her knees.

Max paled under his glossy black hair and turned to Sue. "Er… I think this dog needs to be rested, I'll have to report back!" Before Sue could even speak, he'd turned on his heel and left the room.

George, meanwhile, had approached Maisie to check she was alright. Upon receiving a sneaky wink, his concern was abated but he played along. He said, to nobody in particular, "I think she needs some water. I can help her to the water bowl and sit with her whilst she drinks."

Sue, who had a lot to organise that morning and saw that other dogs had slowed their work rate to watch the unfolding drama, was glad of his offer and nodded her agreement. George escorted a very wobbly Maisie out of the room and into the kitchen to the water bowl.

Lapping quietly at the water bowl, and with no other dogs in the kitchen, Maisie soon made an amazing recovery. "Thank you George, for helping me. I know it's part of the act that we agreed, but it really does show their true colours doesn't it? Time after time, Max tells me I should eat, but then does nothing to help me get food. Then he tells me it's my fault for not trying harder and, when the going gets tough, he disappears!" She waved a paw in the air to demonstrate her point.

George sat quietly and listened to her. He knew she'd finally worked out the pieces for herself, but needed to process the hurt and indignation she felt at Max's treatment of her. He let her talk herself out until finally she gave him a wry smile. "Oh George! I've prattled on havent I? And you are so good to sit with me and listen."

"It's no trouble," he said gruffly. "Gotta watch over the team, y'know." He saw her face fall, just a little, and he could have kicked himself for being just a little too dismissive.

"Yes," she said glumly, "the team." Then, more positively, she continued, "We're a good team and we're going to stop this plan of the Bigs. What can we do next, George?"

The two small dogs sat companionably by the water bowl discussing how they, with their small size, could help foil the Bigs' plan. George suggested it would be madness to try to go back to the work party where Sue would only nip and bully them as she constantly changed her mind about where things were to be put. Instead, they agreed that they would stay by the water bowl where they could speak individually to the dogs of the house as they came for refreshment. They would sound them out to see how they felt about the Bigs' plan and discover what other support they could get for their small group.

So this is what they did. Maisie, looking feeble and wobbly when necessary, continued to sit by the water bowl throughout the day. George solicitously watched over her as she softly chatted with the other house dogs, a few words exchanged here and there. The dogs had been pushed and harassed in their work and felt at ease with the tiny Chihuahua and so she was able to garner a fair amount of information on who would support some sort of 'action'.

The day wore on and Elsie then came to the water bowl. Maisie and George told her what they'd been doing and the information they'd found out. It seemed to them there was a lot of anger at the Bigs. Elsie lapped thoughtfully at the water and raised her eyes to meet Maisie's. "Good work, both of you, it's great to see we have such support. I think we should be cautious, though. The dogs are stressed and angry at the work they're being asked to do today, but whether they would openly defy the Bigs, well that remains to be seen."

She paused as if she heard something and looked around her. Then, satisfied they were still alone, she continued, "I think your work here is done for today. The dogs have sorted the living room out, it's hardly recognisable now! Rumour has it that the human will close the living room door this evening to keep the dogs out and strictly lock the dogs up in the cages tonight so the house is kept tidy until the visit tomorrow. I need you two to be in position in the comfy chair den before that happens. If you follow me into the living room now, I'll see if I can provide a distraction."

The small dogs agreed, took a last lap of water themselves, and followed Elsie out of the kitchen. Luckily, when they arrived at the living room, both Sue and Stu were already engaged with Toby who had just clumsily knocked over a pile of magazines perched on the coffee table. The Bigs had already left the room and so Elsie eagerly joined the fray. She scattered rather than picked up the slippery magazines in her haste to help and drew fresh growls of protest from the Cairns as she did so. George and Maisie slipped quietly into the room behind her, crossed the floor and disappeared into the depths of the comfy chair den unnoticed.

Finally the magazines were sorted and the living room was done. Sue swept a final look around the room, satisfied at last that it would do, then gave a nod to Stu. Together, they started to muster all of the dogs out of the room, before the human closed the door behind them.

It was feeding time next and the weary human doled out the food in the kitchen. The usual mad scramble occurred, with the dogs having worked up quite a hunger during the day and tempers flared as dogs jostled and pushed to get at the food first. Elsie beckoned Norris and Jack to join her in the den under the kitchen units where she explained the rumour about the hard lock down due that night. "We'll all stay here tonight so we don't get locked up, and Jack, you can take up your position in the morning," she said decisively.

Sure enough, as the dogs finished the food, the human started to coerce and pull them into the living room where they were put in cages and the doors locked. They went in ones and twos, depending on size and if they were likely to get on. Toby found himself sharing on the top row with a feisty Yorkshire Terrier called Betsy for which he was glad as he liked both the view and the company. Max was disappointed to find himself stuck on the bottom row and sharing his space with an elderly Jack Russell Terrier called Rogue who seemed to live up to his name, with a shredded ear and scarred face from his days of fighting and chasing rats. Rogue had no time for Max's primping and preening and instead regaled him with long and rambling stories of fights past, his stumpy docked tail wagging at the thought of the catch.

Sue and Stu were swooped up together and locked in a cage on the middle row. This was not to Sue's taste as they were surrounded by dogs in every direction and the noise from top, bottom and each side would make the chances of a night's sleep very slim. She set up a whining noise and received a quick telling off for her efforts, to be a good girl and not fuss.

The Bigs, of course, received special attention and they alone were allowed to stay out and prowl the downstairs spaces. Once the human had gone upstairs for the night, the Bigs stood up and checked out the cages of dogs. Ruby looked over them all approvingly, a wall of scratching, chewing, hairy bodies lined up for her inspection. In her mind, she saw herself as some sort of redeeming mother figure to them all, and she was satisfied with their work that day. The plan was working and the house would be saved. "Good work dogs, just do as we agreed tomorrow and all will be well," she whispered.

Titan liked to go up to the cages and menace the smaller dogs by snarling at the bars, his huge teeth gleaming and his ears flat back, to see who drew back in fear, but tonight Sidney wasn't allowing it. "Come away, Titan, we have things to discuss." The Bigs withdrew, back into the kitchen to have their conversation in private.

Under the kitchen units, Elsie, Norris and Jack sat very still and quiet as they heard the Bigs enter the kitchen. With all the dogs locked away the rest of the house was unusually quiet and so they could hear every word.

"Well that's the house and dogs sorted for now, " gasped Ruby as she sat down and rested her bulging stomach on the cool red kitchen floor tiles, "what's our plan for tomorrow?"

Sidney was restlessly prowling around the kitchen. "We need to make sure Sue and Stu keep the dogs out of the way in the dining room. I've authorised them to use whatever means they must to keep them in there and to make sure they stay quiet. We've got Max primed with the monster story which he can roll out again if we need to frighten them. We can use Toby as an example if any dog needs reminding of what punishment looks like."

Titan sat down by Ruby and grinned, "Yeah! I liked the monster story, that was a nice twist! Max made me chuckle when he told me about Toby wetting himself." He started to laugh.

Ruby shushed him, "Shhh Titan, we don't want the dogs to hear. Yes, the monster story, a brilliant piece of work. It surprised even me how they all fell for it so easily." Changing the subject, she said, "Now back to tomorrow, what are we going to do when the visitors arrive?"

Sidney stopped his prowling for a moment and looked at the other two Bigs and spoke carefully, "We need to control the visit. We must make sure the visitors only go into the living room and they aren't allowed anywhere else in the house. They mustn't see or hear, let alone meet, any other animal. Now, we've already agreed with the cats that they will stay out of the way, and the Cairns will control the dogs in the dining room, so all we need to do is make sure the human obeys our directions."

"The human?" Ruby was surprised. "The human feeds us and looks after us, how will we make the human obey us?"

"There are ways," Sidney stood up very tall and stretched. He really was an impressive looking dog, tall and muscular with a handsome but fierce Doberman face. When he put his ears flat back and opened his jaws he could look very intimidating. He showed his teeth, explaining, "I don't expect to have to use them, but we should be prepared to bully the human into doing what we want. It's for their own good after all." He lowered his voice and continued, "We'll only allow the visitors into the living room and we'll make sure they sit down in the one place and don't get to look around too much. We won't allow them to go nosing around anywhere else and control what they see and do in the living room. We'll make sure the visit is a short one."

"Huh, I can play mean with the visitors alright, but how do we make them leave so soon?" Titan was confused. "We can hardly drag them out of the house?"

"No we can't, but we can control our human." Sidney was expanding on the plan smoothly now. "Ruby can nudge and harass the human as if she needs to go to the toilet and the human won't want that to happen in front of the visitors, so she will get rid of them quickly. We will make sure they leave promptly and go directly out. Titan and I can see to that."

Titan's eyes lit up at that. "Promptly! Yes, I can do that!"

Ruby looked worried, "Boys, you must not bite the humans! We'll all be in big trouble if you do that."

"No, not bite them, exactly, but we'll show our teeth a little and we're big dogs and they won't want to risk it, so they'll do what we want." Sidney was confident the plan would work.

The Bigs continued to talk about their plan until they'd tied up all the loose ends they could think of. Then they slowly moved out of the kitchen to go and lie in the hall for the night, a place where they could keep an eye on movements in the house.

Under the kitchen units, the small dogs were wide-eyed. "We were right," whispered Elsie. "We've got to stop them."

Back in the living room George and Maisie had slipped quietly into the comfy chair den whilst Elsie was providing a distraction with the magazines. They lay, quiet and low, as the dogs were mustered out of the room and a final inspection was made, then finally breathed a sigh of relief as the door was firmly closed. They heard milling around with the usual minor disagreements at tea time and then the house slowly grew quieter as the dogs were locked up in the cages for the night.

They stayed hidden and snoozing in the den until the room grew dark and the only light was a chink of amber street light filtering through the half closed curtains.

His growling stomach prompted George that it was time to eat. "Come on Maisie, let's drag some food out and have a picnic out in the room."

Maisie eagerly agreed and together they wriggled out of the comfy chair, George holding a pouch of chicken flavoured cat food and Maisie with several dog biscuits crammed in her mouth. They dropped down onto the floor and sat on the shabby rug in front of the fireplace. Outside, the grey clouds lifted and the sky cleared. A shaft of white moon light shone onto the rug and lit up a circle in the centre. The two dogs made their way to this place and put their food down.

Maisie was enthralled, "A moonlit picnic, George, how clever! We could dance all night by the stars!" She did a little twirl on the rug.

George bowed, "At your pleasure, Ma'am. But maybe we should eat first?" He chewed at a corner of the cat food pouch until he could tear it open then offered it first to Maisie. "Eat Maisie, I don't want to see you sink to your knees with hunger again."

Maisie looked perplexed, then a look of understanding spread across her petite face. "Oh that! I'd almost forgotten my acting. Did you see the look on Max's face? He couldn't wait to get out of there and leave the problem to Sue. I must say your idea of going to the water bowl was a great inspiration."

George smiled, he'd enjoyed his day with Maisie, the little Chihuahua was brave, fun and always tried to think of others, sometimes to her detriment. Now she needed to eat. "Eat Maisie, it smells delicious, and after we've eaten, we can dance."

Maisie smiled back and started to delicately eat the cat food, the two dogs taking turns to pull at the food and lap up the gravy. Once it was finished, George broke up the biscuits with his teeth and they shared the pieces, chewing softly side by side until they were full.

Maisie sat back, replete. "My, that was good! It's made me thirsty though."

George disappeared back into the comfy chair and returned with a bottle from which he cleverly removed the top and held it on its side for her to lap water from. He watched her drink her fill then he too took a long and much needed drink.

"Now Miss Maisie, may I have the pleasure of the next dance?" The small ginger dog bowed to the petite cream one.

The dogs danced smoothly in the moonlight, Maisie light on her toes, George a supportive and timely partner. They danced silently, each in time with the other, matching their steps and body movements, swaying to the same, imaginary beat. The two small dogs were lost in the moment, enjoying the thrill of their dance.

As the night drew on they grew weary and their steps slowed. After one final slow dance, George guided a weary Maisie to the very centre of the moonlit circle and gruffly whispered, "Lie down Maisie and we'll watch the stars."

Confused, but trusting, Maisie lay down on the threadbare carpet and with George lying beside her, they both looked up. Above them, the grimy living room ceiling was transformed as George described to her the vast black space and the twinkling stars of the starlit night sky. They let their imaginations run wild as they talked on through the night. George pointed out a particularly bright star, over there to her left, and they gasped together as he described a shooting star over to the right. They chatted and mused for hours until they both fell into a deep sleep, dreaming of stars and dancing and moonlit skies.

Chapter Ten

George awoke with a jolt, there were sounds of movement in the house. "Wake up, Maisie, we need to get going!"

Maisie stretched out and yawned. She looked dreamily up at him, then remembered it was the day of the visit and got swiftly to her feet.

"We must hide these things quickly," she said, pointing with her paw to the empty cat food pouch and bottle, "I'll push them under the sofa." She did just that, hiding the evidence of their late night supper under the sprawling green sofa.

George had had an idea during the night. It would be better, he suggested, if they waited in separate dens in the living room and surprised the visitors from two directions. It would be harder for the Bigs to control this situation. Maisie agreed to his plan and offered to take up duty in the sofa if George could arrange a supply of biscuits for her. George readily agreed, disappearing swiftly into the chair den and returning with a mouthful of biscuits for Maisie. Having installed Maisie and her biscuits in the sofa, he returned to the chair den to start his wait. By the sounds of the house waking up, it wouldn't be too long.

Meanwhile, back in the den in the kitchen the other small dogs were also waking up. They too had feasted on the stored food and water, talking quietly and snoozing into the night. They knew the human would feed the animals in the kitchen so they decided to lay low until after breakfast when Jack would make his way to HQ, the den under the stairs.

The human came down the stairs, let the caged dogs out of their prisons and dished out the breakfast food in the kitchen as usual. This morning was different, however. After eating breakfast, the dogs were shooed back into the dining room by the Bigs and Cairns before they could spread out into the house and the Cairns stood guard at the door. The cats put in a brief appearance at breakfast before slinking stealthily away. The Bigs remained in the hall, prowling up and down, keeping a steady eye on the human as she opened the door to the living room and went in to sit down.

The small dogs heard all this play out from inside their den in the kitchen. "We were right," whispered Elsie, "the Bigs are controlling the house."

The morning passed slowly, the human kept looking at the clock and the Bigs alternated between walking around the living room and lying on the floor watching her through half closed eyes.

In their separate living room dens, George and Maisie kept quiet and snoozed the morning away, waiting for the visitors to arrive.

By late morning the house had settled to a quiet uneasiness and Jack realised he still had to get to the den under the stairs to take up his position. He waited until he thought the Bigs and the human were settled down in the living room, then carefully made his way to the hall. He crept past the open living room door, pausing to make sure nobody was watching, then slunk along to the end of the hall to the gap in the boxes. Only this time there was no gap! Somebody had placed a large case down beside the boxes in front of the den, effectively blocking the entrance to small dog HQ.

Jack froze, not quite knowing what to do, and at that moment he heard a step outside the front door as the doorbell was pressed. Fortunately for Jack, the doorbell had long been disconnected which gave him a vital few moments to react before a knock was made on the door and the Bigs and human leapt into action. He had no choice, he couldn't get in the den and he couldn't return past the living room door. Jack turned and bolted in the only direction he could, he ran up the stairs just as a loud rap sounded on the front door and Titan let rip with a throaty bark.

All three Bigs barked at the sound of the knock on the door and followed the human as she went to answer it. On the doorstep stood two female humans, both with name badges attached to lanyards which went round their necks. After a few words of introduction,shouted above the noise of the barking Bigs, the human stood back to allow them into the house. She led the way to the living room with the Bigs shepherding the visitors closely all the way.

When they got to the living room, the human pointed towards the settee and invited the visitors to make themselves comfortable. This they prepared to do, looking closely at the old chewed settee before arranging themselves in front of it all whilst carefully avoiding the various holes. The Bigs stood just to one side, intimidating but friendly for now. Then the human, on edge because of the visit, and impatient to get on with it, said in a loud voice, "Sit!" and they all did. In one sweeping movement, visitors and dogs all sat down and the human herself sat on the comfy chair.

The visitors seemed more settled once the dogs sat. The first one, a fat lady in a blue trouser suit and a white blouse, which she was in danger of spilling out of, started the conversation, "Now Mrs Rogers, my name is Mrs Wright, and my colleague here is Miss Miller." She nodded towards the slim girl with dark tresses who was smoothing a green dress over her knees and looking nervously at the dogs. "We're here to conduct a welfare check on you. That is, we're here to see how you are coping with living on your own and to see if there are any council services we can offer. Miss Miller will ask you some questions and record your answers on the ipad." She motioned with her hand towards her colleague before continuing, "If you could try to answer as best you can, that would be great. Now, do you understand?"

The human nodded and the Bigs glared. The fat lady shifted slightly, there was a lump in the settee underneath where she was sitting which was uncomfortable to sit on and, as she moved, it seemed to move too. She pushed that thought away in her mind, they had three more visits to do that day and she was already hungry, they needed to get on.

Her colleague, Miss Miller, drew out an iPad device from her bag and started to ask some basic questions, tapping out the answers on the screen with a beautifully manicured nail, in green to match her dress. Titan rested his nose on her knee and opened his mouth to reveal a set of gleaming teeth. She started her questions, "Right, er, Mrs Rogers, can you confirm you live here alone?" She squirmed slightly as Titan started to drool.

"Yes dear, since my dear Vernon died I've been all alone," the human said in a croaky voice. "Except for my pets that is."

"Ah yes, your pets, we've had reports of animals on the premises. How many pets exactly do you have?" Miss Miller was looking intently at her ipad and tapping things into it.

"Ooh!" the fat lady wriggled in her seat. The lump was back. Her colleague looked enquiringly at her but she shrugged and kept her eyes on the large Doberman which had got to its feet and sauntered over towards her.

Miss Miller repeated her question,"Mrs Rogers, how many pets?" She raised her eyes to look at her.

"Well I'm not very good with numbers you know. There's Titan here, but you've met him haven't you?" That was certainly true as his drool was starting to wet Miss Miller's dress and dribble down her leg. "And then there's my lovely Ruby here..." Ruby, at least, was behaving impeccably, sitting beside her owner and watching carefully with big brown eyes. "Then there's my big boy Sidney, he's got papers you know."

"Are they all the pets you have?" Miss Miller valiantly continued with her questions and stared at a small mound of fluff which seemed to be moving next to where the human was sitting.

"Pets ha! Those were the days. Vernon used to breed them you know and show them too..." The human's voice trailed off and her eyes glazed over, looking at something far away in her memories.

"Ah!" The fat lady was sure she felt the lump move this time. She shifted on her ample behind and tried to focus on the human. "Mrs Rogers, if you could answer the questions truthfully, we won't take up much more of your time. Are these three dogs all the pets you have?"

"There's sometimes a couple of cats that come in to eat, but I don't have much to do with them," the human added. The Bigs relaxed, she was playing her part.

"So I'll put that down as three dogs and two cats?" Miss Miller looked over at her to check. *What was that thing moving?* She shook her head, she too was hungry and keen to get on.

The human nodded and the Bigs imperceptibly drew back, the visit was drawing to a close, their work was nearly done.

In the comfy chair, George decided he'd had enough, the visit was going according to the Bigs' plan. He had already popped his head up through the chair's stuffing beside the human to hear better what was being said, but now it was time to act. As Miss Miller tapped the final letters into her iPad and looked up to meet the human's eyes, he briefly pushed his ginger nose and whiskers up out of the chair.

"Eeek!" squeaked Miss Miller. "What was that?" She stared at the spot where a set of ginger whiskers had appeared.

"What was what dearie?" The human was unconcerned.

"That, that hairy thing underneath you!" Miss Miller's voice was high pitched now as she pointed at the comfy chair with one hand and waved the iPad high with the other.

Titan was alerted now at the sound of Miss Miller's squeal and the gesticulating of her arms, and he stood up and gave out a low pitched growl. Miss Miller froze.

Maisie had heard the signal. She had endured the heavy weight of the fat visitor sitting on top of her and heard the lies being told. Well, now she had her chance. Infuriated at the fibbing, she reached up with her mouth and opened her small jaw wide. She took aim, and bit as hard as she could on the ample bottom sitting on the settee.

"Aaaargh!" The fat lady had felt the lump squirming beneath her but, before she could move, she had felt the sharp pain of the nip. "I've been bitten!". She jumped up all flustered and stared at the settee where she had been sitting and rubbed a sore spot on her ample behind. Both of the visitors looked wildly about them but the human simply sat there looking confused and Titan looked more menacing than ever.

Hastily now, and keeping an eye on the big dogs, the fat lady gathered up her bag, "I think we've wasted enough of your time, Mrs Rogers, and we need to get on. Thank you for your time today. Miss Miller, are you ready?"

Miss Miller wasted no time either. The iPad was stowed back in her bag and she too was on her feet, eyes warily tracking where Titan stood. "I'm finished here, let's go."

They walked towards the living room door and out into the hall, escorted solemnly by the Bigs, who were hoping they'd got away with their deceit. The visitors were just saying their goodbyes when a blood curdling scream stopped them all in their tracks.

Chapter Eleven

Jack had bolted up the stairs, away from the hall where the Bigs were now marching the human to meet the visitors at the door. He turned at the top of the stairs and ran across the landing and through the only open door. Safe, for now, he stopped and looked around.

The room was in semi darkness since the curtains were still closed so he could just make out some of the furniture. The middle of the room was taken up by a big double bed with the bed clothes still ruffled from the night before and there was a dressing table by the window upon which piles of nik naks and bottles stood. On the floor were more piles, this time piles of clothes, books and dirty cups. Jack realised he'd run into the human's bedroom.

He made his way around the bed. It was too tall for him to jump on directly, but he thought that if he could just locate something to use as a step, he might be able to make it. Wary, because he'd never been in the room before, but eyeing up the softness of the bed, he thought he could burrow down there and wait until the visitors left.

Finding a pile of large books stacked close to the foot of the bed, he climbed on top of them, and stood wobbling for a moment before making a big leap onto the bed itself. Once on top, he found a comfortable spot in the middle where he nestled down into the bed clothes and curled up to wait it out.

"What have we got here?" A dark shape came to life and, as Jack raised his head to look, a pair of green eyes opened to look at him.

Jack started and sat up suddenly, "W...w...what? Who's there?"

"Sss...somebody's where he sssshouldn't be" Another dark shape opened its eyes.

"We have a visitor." A third pair of eyes opened and looked at him. Jack was surrounded by the cats and he was in their lair.

"N...n...now then ladies, er, good morning," he croaked. "No offence meant, I thought you'd, er, all gone outside..."

"Outside?" The first cat, Izzy, was outraged. "Outside, why would we go outside?"

"Well, you know, what with the visitors and stuff." Jack shrugged, his brain was working overtime. The cats were vicious and here he was caught right in the middle of their lair and they didn't look very happy. *Perhaps*, he thought, *if I can distract them, they'll leave me alone.*

"Visssitorsss?" lisped the second cat, Lizzie.

"Yes, you know the council visitors, they've come to do the welfare check," Jack replied, keeping a wary eye on the dark shapes and hoping he could keep them talking until they let him go.

"And how do you know about the council and the welfare check?" The third cat, Kizzy, was quick to jump in and she stretched out a sharply clawed paw as she spoke.

"Yes, how do you know about that?" Izzy looked at him, her green eyes narrowing to study him closely. "Only we cats knew that and we told the Bigs on condition they kept it to themselves."

The cats were closer now and the hair on the back of Jack's neck stood up with fear. He had to think quickly. "Er, a dog told me, I forget who."

"Tell ussss who told you!" Lizzie hissed and she swiped at his tail with her sharp claws, just grazing the end.

Jack promptly tucked his tail and ears down and out of the way. "I really can't remember," he said and as the cats edged ever closer, he tried a different tack. "Now ladies, I'm sure there's no need for violence, if you would just let me go then I can ask around the dogs and get right back to you." He looked hopefully at Izzy.

His attempt to appease the cats hadn't worked, in fact it seemed to make them even angrier. As he looked around at the faces glaring at him, he realised that all three had unsheathed their claws and were preparing to pounce.

"Get him girls!" shouted an infuriated Izzy and the cats sprang forward.

Jack closed his eyes and screamed at the top of his voice, "Ow, wow, wow, wow, ow!" He curled up tightly into a ball as the cats attacked him, biting and scratching and pulling at his fur.

He didn't know how long the attack lasted. It seemed like ages, but it was only a few moments before he heard the sound of feet running up the stairs and the door to the bedroom being flung open.

"My goodness, what's going on here?" gasped an out of breath human as the cats ran for the door and swiftly disappeared.

Mrs Wright had heard the scream and, acting purely on impulse, had bounded up the stairs two at a time, a fact she was now regretting as she gasped for breath. She had rushed to the front bedroom and thrust the door open, flooding the room with light and illuminating the horror scene before her. Three cats were lashing out at a small white bundle on the bed, clumps of white hair flying up and from which an unearthly screeching noise was emanating.

The cats, disturbed by the light and the sound of a hefty human clumping into the room, quickly vanished, slithering off the bed in three directions and scooting out of the room.

The small clump of white hair shook and shivered in the middle of the bed as the fat lady sat down beside it and slowly picked it up. "You poor creature," she whispered as she looked down at it.

Jack was, indeed, a poor creature. He allowed himself to be picked up and carefully examined. He had great tufts of fur missing, several bleeding scratches on his face and body, his tail was tucked between his back legs and several fleas could be seen crawling in his white fur.

The lady put him gently down again on the bed and stood up. "Mrs Rogers!" she called. "Mrs Rogers, a word if you will."

Jack sat shivering as he heard the clumping of more human feet on the stairs and then the human and another young woman, who he assumed was the other visitor, came into the bedroom.

"Mrs Rogers, this poor animal has been attacked by cats and needs attention!" The fat lady drew herself up to her full height and spluttered, "the animal also seems to have f… fleas!"

The human looked vaguely at Jack, uncomprehending but nodding anyway.

"Mrs Rogers, it appears you have more animals than you told us about and it seems there may be a safety concern regarding them. I will have to put this in my report and we may take further action. Do you understand?"

The human stood mutely, still gazing at Jack, then she picked him up and crooned to him like a baby, rocking him in her arms.

"We've seen enough for now, if you would be so good as to see us out?" The fat lady was at her most officious now.

"Yes, yes, this way." The human led the visitors out of the bedroom and down the stairs to the front door, still holding Jack in her arms. The Bigs were waiting in the hall, but the fat lady pushed her way through them and put her hand out to grasp the catch to open the door.

As she did so, two small bundles of fur came charging out of the kitchen and screeched to a halt in front of her. "Woof, woof!" they shouted, and the larger of the two jumped up at Miss Miller, nearly causing her to drop her bag in surprise.

"More animals?" The fat lady was unamused. "Mrs Rogers, you'll be hearing from us," she said. Wiith a slick turn of the handle she flung open the door and ushered Miss Miller and her bag out. The two visitors trod swiftly down the front path and clanged the gate shut behind them, shuddering as an even louder chorus of dog barking broke out.

Back in the house, the human sat down on the stairs with Jack on her lap and cried silent tears as she stroked him over and over. Jack sat quietly, his wounds smarting, and licked her face.

Part Two - Trouble

Chapter Twelve

Jack was dreaming again. He lay in the lap of the human, listening to her sobbing quietly. He dreamt of the time after his mother had disappeared, when the human had gathered him up and quietly stroked him, all whilst speaking meaningless words to him as he mourned for her loss. Those had been special times and he'd gained huge comfort from the comforting lap and soft stroking movements.

"What on earth did you think you were doing?" The high pitched, angry voice was close by and woke him up with a start. Sue was standing by the stairs with an annoyed look on her face. The human reached out to her too but Sue was having none of it and slid away from under her hand. "You've messed things up properly this time, Jack. The visit was a disaster. I don't doubt we'll all be turned out of the house to face the monsters after this!"

The human got slowly to her feet, putting Jack down on the stairs and walked slowly towards the kitchen. She had tea to prepare after all. Sue continued with her lecturing of Jack for a while but soon the usual cacophony of dogs barking and whining for food started and Sue turned her attention to her tea. Leaving Jack sitting at the bottom of the stairs, she walked off down the hall towards the kitchen.

"Jack? Jack help me move this box?" It was Elsie's voice and she was standing beside the box that blocked the way into the small dogs' HQ. Jack turned and together they pushed the box out of the way of the small gap, then Elsie nudged Jack to follow her and they both squeezed into the den.

Once in the den, Elsie looked carefully at Jack. He certainly looked a sight, with clumps of hair missing and patches of drying blood from the scratches making red streaks across his face and body. He was still shaking uncontrollably from the trauma. Elsie sat close to him sharing her body warmth and slowly helped him lick his wounds clean and tidy up his fur. When he was more presentable, Elsie pointed towards the small pile of food and water in the corner. "Shall we have some supper, Jack? I think you've earned it," she said and the two small dogs ate and drank in companionable silence and Jack's shaking slowly subsided.

One by one, the rest of the small dogs slowly found their way into HQ where, upon entering the den, all of them sniffed and touched noses with Jack to check he was alright before sitting down and sharing some biscuits.

When they were all assembled and the biscuits eaten, Elsie called the meeting to order. The small dogs sat watching her as she stood and faced them and smiled ruefully. "Well the plan didn't go quite as expected but I think we got a result. It seems that we foiled the Bigs' plan and the visitors got more information to take away with them than they bargained for. I'd like to thank you all for your hard work in making it happen, but special praise goes to Jack who braved the wrath of the cats and whose actions probably swung the whole visit in our favour."

The small dogs all nodded in agreement and Jack looked suitably embarrassed because he knew he hadn't been brave at all. Still, those bumps and scratches had to count for something, didn't they?

Elsie continued, "Now we must be on our guard. The Bigs have noticed us and are suspicious. I think they may look for retribution of some kind, we will need to be careful."

Again the nodding and mumbled agreement, then Maisie spoke up, "How will we stay safe? You saw what they did to poor Toby and now Jack. We are, after all, so very small."

Even more agreement, but this time a shaking of the heads as the dogs contemplated the revenge the Bigs might want to exact.

Elsie sensed the real fear in the small dogs. "I know you're frightened, but we've just proven what even small dogs can do if we work as a team. We will only beat them if we stick together. We must look out for each other and never let them divide us."

The small dogs looked doubtful, but George, seeing the sense of Elsie's argument, slowly nodded his ginger head. "Elsie's right. Look at how we helped Toby and foiled the Bigs' plot for the visit. Just five small dogs and we stuck together and made it work."

More positive rumblings, except Jack who sat quietly in the group. He looked at the others and whispered, "You're mostly right, Elsie, except..., well..., except they'll be coming back for me."

Elsie put her head on one side. "I don't understand, the cats punished you for going into their lair and the Bigs will just be annoyed that you very publicly spoiled their plan. Why would they come back especially for you?"

Jack had started to shake again. "Those cats, they threatened me and I was frightened and... and I let slip that I knew where the visitors were from and why they had come. They wanted to know who had told me, but I wouldn't tell them, I couldn't betray you all. But they'll tell the Bigs and they'll want to know who informed on their plan." He gulped, "They'll torture me until they get the information. Next time there won't be any visitors to save me."

Norris had been listening with his head on one side. He smiled as a thought struck him. "It's simple really. You you just tell them it was Max, then they'll leave you alone."

"But that wouldn't be true and besides, what has Max done to deserve the punishment they'll mete out?" Jack wasn't happy, frowning and looking down at his paws as he spoke.

"But Norris has a point, it would stop the cats hurting you." It was Maisie, speaking softly, "and he did tell me about the plot so it would only be a half lie."

"Yes," piped up George, "and I'm sure our Max can talk his way out of things, he has a knack of doing that. Why would you protect him?"

"And look at how Max treated Toby," Elsie too expanded on the idea. "Why, he told Maisie that he'd laughed at his own 'monsters' joke and how frightened it had made Toby."

Jack was still frowning. "I suppose you're all right, but I'm just not comfortable with it. I don't like the idea of getting someone else into trouble."

"Let's leave it for now then," said Elsie sensibly, "we'll try to protect you by never leaving you on your own. However, if you must, and as a last resort, then we're agreed you can name Max."

The small dogs were tired after a busy day, so having eaten and agreed a way forward, they settled down to sleep in small-dog HQ.

All was quiet except for the sounds of dogs breathing as they slept, then slowly the whimpering and twitching of paws started. Jack was having a dream again and his paws were moving as, in his dream, he ran away from devil cats with glaring, green eyes and scratching, scraping claws. "Help me!" he screamed as a wet tongue slid down his ear.

"Jack, wake up!" It was Elsie licking his ear. "Jack, it's just a nightmare, wake up!"

"What?" Jack was trembling again, but he could feel the body warmth of Elsie next to him. He felt her soft tongue smoothing down his fur around the sore scratches on his face and body. "Oh, Elsie, the cats were coming to get me in my sleep!"

"They won't get you as long as we small dogs stick together, now you can sleep," Elsie replied. Her warmth and rhythmic licking soon had its intended effect and Jack slipped back into sleep, but this time without the bad dreams.

Chapter Thirteen

Saturday morning dawned, cool and quiet. The house came to life bit by bit, in the same pattern as usual. There was the sound of the human slowly getting out of bed and moving around before descending the stairs and letting the locked up dogs out of the cages. With dragging feet, she went into the kitchen and filled and switched on the kettle, then walked over to the pantry door which she opened and, pushing back excited dog noses, she fetched out several pouches of cat food and a large bag of dog food crunchies.

The food was dispensed as always, cats fed first on the worktop where they sniffed it suspiciously, ate a small mouthful or two, then disappeared outside. They had better things to do than eat cat food , they would hunt for prey first, then return.

Next the dog food was doled out in huge handfuls into bowls and plates and these were put down on the floor. The hungry dogs fought furiously over the food, with the larger dogs pushing in first and grabbing the majority of the food. As they got fuller and ate more slowly, the smaller or weaker dogs pushed in to grab some of the food and crept away to eat in peace.

The small dogs, having slept in HQ all night, snuck into the kitchen den, watched the mayhem and bided their time. Once the main scrum was over and the Bigs and Cairns had left the room, the small dogs crept out to start eating the dog food.

Their friend Toby, distracted and late as always, was still there, chomping away on a dog crunchy. "Hello you guys, where have you been? There's going to be a reckoning after yesterday."

Elsie smiled at him. "I don't know what you mean, Toby," she said smoothly, "I thought the visit went rather well."

"Well you should have been in lockup all night like I was. The human put me in with Stu and Sue was put in the next cage. When they thought I was asleep, the Cairns couldn't stop talking between themselves, I heard it all..." His voice became muffled as he came across a small pile of crunchies and hoovered them up in one go. He chewed and swallowed, before continuing, "It seems the Bigs are fuming. Their carefully made plan didn't work and now there may be repercussions. Jack, your name was mentioned a lot."

"Oh?" Jack pricked up his Chi ear. "What do you mean, repercussions?"

Toby scoffed another mouthful of crunchies, swallowed and sat down to tell the tale. It seemed the Bigs had been aware of the small dogs' attempted interventions. However, they put these down to the fact that the little dogs were always popping in and out of the dens looking for food or someone to annoy and so they had dismissed these as simply a nuisance and not a planned attack. There was no plan by the Bigs to take things further.

The small dogs visibly relaxed at this. It was good news, but Toby continued his tale. Jack was another matter. The Bigs had heard the scream and followed the visitors to the hall where the human had prevented them from following the fat lady upstairs. Instead they had listened to the commotion and witnessed the cats fleeing at high speed, followed by the return of the visitors with Jack in the human's arms. They had watched as their plan fell to pieces as words were exchanged and the visitors swiftly left. They had seen their human slumped and crying on the stairs with a small, bedraggled Jack on her knee.

The story of the cats' attack had been gleaned from an outraged Lizzie later that afternoon when the cats had judged it safe to return. She had bumped into Ruby who had been waiting in the hall hoping to catch up with the cats and told her that Jack had 'inssssside information', with the cats simply trying to obtain the name of the informer. The Bigs were concerned about this news, it had now become imperative for them to find out who the informer was. They would need to question Jack themselves and had tasked Sue and Stu to bring him in.

"Jack you need to be careful," Toby said, his glorious golden ears drooping, "they sounded really angry about this, I'm worried for you."

"I know," Jack acknowledged sadly, "they'll be gunning for me now, but what can a small dog do?"

"Nonsense! We have our plan to protect you Jack." Elsie, practical as always, was not going to be defeated just yet and she quickly outlined to Toby their plan not to leave Jack on his own. "They'll find it harder to get to him if we work together, will you help us?"

Toby readily agreed, after all he was indebted to all the small dogs for helping him when he was punished and anyway, Jack was his friend.

So, for the rest of the day the small dogs and their friend, Toby, played a peculiar game of protecting Jack. He was accompanied and guarded by a stream of small dogs who kept a lookout to move him safely from den to den. They found and fed him biscuits and fallen cat crunchies and Norris even found his sock toy so they could indulge in a game of tug of war with it.

The house was subdued, with dogs whispering in corners and the human sitting on the sofa, staring sightlessly at the clock and carefully guarded by the Bigs. The Cairns prowled restlessly from room to room as though they were looking for something or someone.

At tea time the feeding ritual began again and the dogs crowded into the small kitchen to argue over the dog biscuits and crunchies as they were dished out. Jack stayed hidden in the den under the kitchen units whilst the other small dogs joined the throng once the main rush had died away. The human had been distracted and had forgotten to put the last dish of crunchies down. There it sat, up high on the worktop where none of the smaller dogs could reach it and below on the kitchen floor there was not a crunchy or biscuit left for the small dogs. They returned to the kitchen den to plan.

Elsie was impatient. "How annoying, we'll need to get some more food from the pantry. Norris, you can stay with Jack and then George and Maisie can come with me to fetch some food."

The small dogs nodded. "Come on then!" She was gone, her small legs padding purposefully along as she marched out of the kitchen. George looked at Maisie, shrugged and then they followed her, trotting to keep up.

Jack looked at Norris in the gloom. "Just us now," he said and slowly scratched his ear. He was still in pain from the attack by the cats so he winced as he caught a sore spot. He tried to rub his itchy ear on the chewed corner of the plinth but didn't have much success that way either.

The flash of white fur under the kitchen unit had been spotted though, Max lay quietly in the hallway and waited.

Norris hated waiting and Jack was restless and itchy too. His beloved sock was in the other den so instead he nipped Norris who nipped him back and pushed him until they were in a mock fight tussle.

"Ouch!" Jack finally exclaimed. "That hurts!" They stopped the fight and sat looking at each other.

Norris sat for a minute and tried really hard to be still, then gave up. "I know what we need, I'll fetch sock then we can play without you hurting, that'll also take your mind off the itching. Don't worry, you'll be safe enough here, I won't be long." Before Jack could reply he was gone, out of the den and along the hall.

He didn't see the dark shape waiting out there, he was so focussed on fetching the sock and getting back quickly. Max sat and watched as Norris ducked between some boxes and disappeared under the stairs. He followed and pushed a large and hefty box in front of where he had seen Norris disappear, that would give him some time. Quietly now, Max went back to the kitchen doorway and lay down. He waited.

Jack sat under the units also waiting. His ear was sore and itchy, he was getting thirsty and Norris was taking forever. *Where was he?* He decided to look out into the kitchen. It was dark out there, but the room was empty and Jack was starting to get very thirsty indeed. He could just make out the shape of the water bowl and he could imagine the cool delicious water there. He listened, but all was quiet, so he made up his mind and slipped out from the den and scurried over to the water bowl to take a long drink. *Ooh that was better.*

He finished his lapping and turned round, ready to return to the den, but there was a dark shape blocking his path. "Hello Jack," said Max smoothly, "I think the Bigs are looking for you."

Jack froze and started to wonder how he was going to talk his way out of this, when, to his horror, Max started to bark. "Woof, woof," he barked, "come quick, look who's here!"

Instantly, there came the sound of large paws pounding towards the kitchen and Jack knew he was doomed. He couldn't get around Max to get to the den and his friends had disappeared. He stood on the kitchen floor and started to shake.

Max's rallying call brought the Bigs running in first, followed by the Cairns trotting along behind and then, finally, the cats slid into the kitchen. They formed a menacing circle around Jack and the water bowl. Max bowed to the Bigs and slunk out of the kitchen. He'd be able to say he had had no part in the proceedings when asked, Jack was disgusted at his cowardice. But Max couldn't resist wanting to know what was going to happen so he stopped at the kitchen bin and hid behind it.

Sidney was the first to speak, "Good evening, Jack, we've been searching for you. I think you know why."

Jack bravely stalled for time, hoping desperately that his friends would somehow manage to rescue him. "Me? Looking for me? Why, er, would that be? I'm just a small dog." Indeed he was a very tiny dog, shrunk back towards the water bowl and looking wide eyed at the surrounding circle of Bigs, Cairns and cats.

Sidney sighed, he was losing patience already. "You know what I mean, you broke the rules. Stu! Interrogate the prisoner if you please," he barked.

"Yes Sir! Certainly Sir!" Stu stepped forward and puffed out his shaggy chest. He stepped right up to Jack, who quivered even harder, and started to bark out the offences listed against him. "One. Breaking the lockup arrangements for the visit as mandated by the dog council. Two. Going upstairs and entering the cats' lair. Three. Withholding information on an informant contrary to the dog council's plan. Four. Liaising with a visitor to the house without permission." Stu's whiskers bristled with indignation as he read out the charges. "Jack, how do you plead?"

Jack shook even harder but bravely replied, "this is all a mistake, I was confused and didn't mean any harm."

"How do you plead?" It was Titan, pushing his face towards Jack now, his lips drawn back to reveal his huge teeth.

"N...n...not guilty Sir!" The small dog valiantly forced the words out.

"Huh, the case against you is proven, we have witnesses, cats if you please?" Stu looked round at the cats and signalled them to step forward.

Izzy was the first to speak, her green eyes narrowed and glittering as she looked at Jack. "Yes indeed. Well, we cats were sleeping in our lair, out of the way of the visitors just as agreed at the dog council, when Jack came into the bedroom and jumped up onto the bed. When we politely asked him what he was doing there, he said he thought we'd gone outside and that he'd come up to avoid the visitors whilst they carried out the welfare check. We knew that information was strictly confidential and we asked him where he got it from..." She paused for a moment as if trying to find the right words.

"He wouldn't tell us and instead started screaming to get the attention of the visitors, who came up to see what the fuss was about. We disappeared at that point as we had instructions not to engage with the visitors. Jack not only stayed but put on an act so the visitors would believe he was being mistreated!" Izzy looked around at the other two cats.

"Yesss he ssscreamed to get the visssitorsss' attention and tried to blame usss," Lizzie chimed in and Kizzy nodded.

Ruby also added her voice. "It seems a pretty clear cut case," she remarked, "but how did Jack know about the welfare check? That was only known by a few privileged animals, how did he find out about it?"

Stu turned to Jack. "Who told you? Who gave you the information?"

Jack was terrified, he'd heard the cats twist the story and knew they were after his blood. He could see Titan, ready to use those enormous jaws of his to hold him down and the cats unsheathing their sharp claws, ready to strike. He thought of how Max had caught him and reported him to the Bigs and realised he was protecting a dog who cared only for himself. He made his decision. "M...M..Max…" he whispered.

"What? What did you say? Speak louder so we can all hear." Stu was close now.

Jack tilted his head up and met his eye. "Max! It was Max who told me! He was showing off and told me he knew about the visit." There, the part lie was out, they would let him go now.

"Max? Come, come now, you don't expect us to believe that?" It was Sue, closing in from the other side. "Why would Max tell you anything?"

Jack kept his head. "It's true, it was Max. He told me the other day when he was trying to impress… to impress... me." *Careful now, careful not to involve anyone else.*

Sue stared hard at him, then apparently satisfied, she shrugged. "He could be telling the truth, it's hard to tell."

"Let usssss try. We'll get it out of him, if you pleasssse." Lizzie sidled closer and Jack involuntarily shrank back.

"Enough!" Sidney took back control and growled, "He's told us what he knows and we'll deal with that later. I think a night in solitary will allow him to reflect on his deeds, Sue, Stu you can enact the punishment, I hereby close this hearing." He looked at Ruby and Titan. "Come, we have other things to do." The three

Bigs drew themselves up to their full heights, glared around at the other animals, then left the kitchen.

Jack stood between the Cairns, shaking still but less intensely. The cats threw him one final look of loathing, then slid out of the room in the direction of their lair.

Jack sat quietly between Sue and Stu. He was somewhat relieved and meekly complied when they pushed him toward the door that led into the attached garage. As they paused by the unlatched door to allow Stu to reach his paw around to open it wider, a black shape reentered the kitchen. "Watch out for the monsters, Jack," Max whispered as he slid away, laughing to himself.

Monsters indeed! Jack knew he had faced his monsters bravely, he wondered if Max would be so bold when they caught up with him.

The Cairns led him into the dim garage and Stu pushed the box forward from under the table to allow Jack to climb up into the hutch. Jack didn't resist, what was the point? Stu closed the latch to the prison as he said, "Now Jack, you behave lad. Nice and quiet for the night now. Time to reflect upon your crimes, we'll be back for you in the morning."

Jack slowly nodded and watched the shaggy shapes of the Cairns retreat across the garage and disappear through the door to the kitchen. He lay down in the hutch, he was suddenly very weary after his long and scary day.

Chapter Fourteen

Norris had returned to small dog HQ. His eyes carefully scanned the hall then he slipped into the gap between the boxes and rubbish and crept into the den under the stairs. He didn't hear or notice Max follow him nor did he notice him push the heavy box until it blocked the entrance, he was intent on finding the sock toy for Jack. Inside the den he met Elsie who was watching as George and Maisie worked to fetch food, one each side of the hole into the pantry. Dog biscuits and pouches of cat food were being pushed through from beyond the wall by a tiny but determined Maisie and George was receiving and neatly stacking them. He stopped briefly to nod to Norris, then heard a call from the other side and resumed his work.

Elsie offered a biscuit. "What's up Norris, why have you come here?" She checked behind him, saying, "Where's Jack? Have you left him alone?"

Norris chewed down and swallowed the biscuit. "Jack's fine, I left him safe in the kitchen den and there's nobody around. He's just itching and scratching and fretting about stuff so I came to get the sock toy for him. Ahh yes, there it is!" He spied the sock in the corner, behind the growing pile of biscuits, and picked it up. "I see you've all been busy! Well keep up the good work, I'd better get back." He turned to exit the den.

His nose bumped into the box that had been pushed by Max to block the den's entrance. "That's funny, I'm sure that wasn't there when I came in," he muttered. He pushed at the box with his nose, it didn't move. He put the sock down, then pushed again, still no movement. He wriggled in the tight space until he could get his shoulder against the box and shoved with all his might. No change.

He heard Elsie behind him. "What's the matter, Norris, why can't you get out?"

He tried pulling back and bashing at the box, but that didn't work either. "It's blocked, there's a heavy box blocking the entrance and I can't shift it."

George and Maisie had finished fetching the food supplies and Maisie had wriggled back into the den. George was keen to try. "Back up Norris, I'll give it a go, see if I can make it budge." The two small dogs squeezed past each other and swapped places. George tried to move the box, he pushed it, rammed it, tried to rock it, but still it stood firm. After several minutes of heavy work, he sat back down, panting. "No, Norris was right, it's blocked, we can't get out."

"But what about Jack? If we are trapped, how can we protect him?" Maisie was worried.

"Norris said he left him in the kitchen den so he should be safe for now, we'll just have to think of another way to get out of here." Elsie was realistic as usual. "Maisie, you're the smallest, is there any way you could wriggle out of here?"

"Let me have a look," said Maisie, swapping places with George. There was a wall of solid cardboard in front of her but she could see a chink of light up to the top right and thought that if she could just get to that she might be able to wriggle through. There was only one thing to do, she started to chew and scratch at the cardboard.

She sank her sharp teeth into the highest corner she could reach and pulled with all her might. A tiny strip of paper came off. She tried again and pulled a similar piece off. Again and again she tore at the cardboard, teeth and claws slowly widening the hole to the light.

It was slow progress and, after a while, she stopped for a rest and to let George take her place. The small dogs took it in turns to take their place and tear at the box, Norris next and then Elsie. Elsie made some good progress when a chunk of cardboard she was chewing at gave way and she found herself with a clearer view out beyond the box. The hole was still far too small to wriggle through, but she could see a little way out and hear sounds from the hall beyond.

She heard a snuffle out in the hall and then saw a glimpse of golden hair. "Toby?" she whispered, "Is that you, Toby?"

It was indeed Toby. "Yes it's me," he replied, " What's the matter? I heard scratching."

"Toby, we're stuck behind this box, can you help us?" Elsie was hopeful.

"I'll try!" The golden hair disappeared from view. A few moments later the box rocked a little and then shook before slowly starting to move as Toby put a shoulder to it and started to push it out of the way.

Now Elsie could see Toby's face clearly. "Thank you Toby, thank you so much! We were all trapped. Somebody must have moved that box to keep us in there." She paused then added, "It's not safe, Toby, perhaps you'd better go now before the Bigs come."

Toby grinned. "Not much chance of that at the moment, they've got Jack caught in the kitchen, they won't be bothering us for a bit." He saw her face fall and the worried expression return. "Don't worry, they're holding some sort of pseudo court to try him, but I doubt they'll go too far. Whispers are that he's named Max, it's Max who should be worried." He cocked an ear to listen. "Still, it sounds like they're wrapping things up, I'll leave you now." The golden hair disappeared from view.

As Elsie breathed a sigh, a flash of black caught her eye and she saw the three cats slinking past the den on their way to climb the stairs to their lair, shortly followed by the Bigs who looked like they were looking for someone. *At least that threat to Jack has been removed*, she thought, then turned to relay the news to the rest of the small dogs.

"What do you think they'll do with Jack now?" Norris wanted to know.

"My guess is they'll put him out of the way for a while, probably in solitary. They'll want to make a statement to the other dogs, to warn them about disobeying orders. If we wait a while we can check and see if he's alright..." Elsie was interrupted by the sounds of a commotion out in the hall and then a howl.

The small dogs sat very quietly, they had recognised the voice of Max and guessed correctly that the Bigs had caught up with him. They could hear sounds of a scuffle in the hall outside the den and Max loudly protesting his innocence as his body was beset with bites and blows.

"Bad dogs! Now stop it! Titan sit!" The sound of footsteps swiftly approaching, then the exasperated voice of the human, broke into the kerfuffle. "Bad dogs fighting! You'll all be the death of me, come here now it's time out time". The small dogs listened intently and heard noises of someone dragging dogs out of the hall and towards the dining room, where more distant sounds could be heard of cages being opened and then closed and locked. Then they heard more dogs being called and cages banging shut.

"It's a complete lock up tonight," Elsie whispered. "Sounds like the human's really fed up with the fighting this time. Best lay low here for a while."

She was right, the human caught all the dogs and pushed them into the cages. "Bad dogs, no more fighting tonight!" Even the Bigs were pushed into separate cages on the bottom row, their bodies crammed in and barely fitting the space. The Cairns were caged together on top, but smaller dogs were crushed willy nilly into other cages, two or three dogs per cage. Max, who was bleeding from several bite wounds and was holding up a paw, found himself put into a cage with Toby near to the door.

The human stood back and surveyed her work, a tear of frustration rolling down her cheek. "After all I do for you dogs too, well you can have a night without fighting now." Then she left the dining room, closing the door to behind her and walked slowly upstairs.

The cats had heard the commotion downstairs and wisely hid themselves under the bed. The house grew quiet as darkness descended and the animals settled, each finding a place to lie down and wait out the long night to come.

Out in the garage in the prison hutch, Jack also heard the commotion inside the house. Like the rest of the small dogs, he too lay quiet and low, hoping not to be discovered. He too waited for darkness and quiet to fall on the house. As he lay there, occasionally scratching at his fleas, he dozed and dreamed.

He dreamed of his mother, a tiny Chihuahua who had taught him how to live in a world in which he would always be the smallest. Feisty herself, she had been ready to defend her puppies with a snarl and a snap, but was loving and kind to those she cherished. She had fed him and taught him how to play in the sunlight when the leaves on the trees outside had cast dappled patterns through the windows. Jump, pounce, snarl. The shadows moved quickly, try it again.

She had been devastated when, one by one, her puppies had been removed, until it was just her and Jack left. Jack had practised the jump, pounce, snarl. They wouldn't separate him from his mother. But one day, he had been playing with his cousin, Norris, and got shut in another room. When he looked for his mother, she had gone. No goodbye, just gone. Jack had looked everywhere and asked everyone he knew about her, but she had simply disappeared.

Jack had mourned for her, unhappily pining and forgetting to eat. That was when the human had sat with him, taking him onto her knee and crooning to him, feeding him tasty little titbits. Slowly the waves of grief had passed and Jack resumed his life, looking for food and playing with Norris. But he never forgot either the jump, pounce, snarl his mother had taught him nor the kindness and security of the human's lap.

He woke from his dream, it was now fully dark outside with just a glimmer of street light filtering into the garage and the house itself was quiet. He knew he had to make his move, the monsters were no threat to him, they didn't exist, but the Bigs and the cats? Yes, there was danger there, *better get moving before they came back for him.*

He stood up in the hutch and pushed at the front of the cage, it didn't move. He remembered the latch, just outside, about halfway up. He used his long, long tongue to feel for it, *ah yes, there it was.* He pushed at it with his tongue and it started to move, he pushed some more and finally the latch was clear and the door started to open. He pushed at the door with his nose and it swung wide and he stepped out of his prison.

Jack stood on the table and spotted the box below. The Cairns had been in such a hurry to finish and get back to the house, they'd left his step out. He jumped down, one, two, onto the garage floor and made his way over to the grill to the pantry. Standing on the box below it, he realised he had a problem. The cover for the grill opened outwards and Maisie wasn't there to keep it open whilst he jumped up. He tried to push it open with his nose, but it sprang back. He tried again, trying to wedge it open with his paw and scrambling for the gap, but that didn't work either, he needed a clear gap to jump through. "Help!" he called despairingly, "Maisie, where are you?"

Then he heard a faint voice. "Jack! Hold on Jack, I'm coming!" A few moments later the grill was pushed open by a cream paw and Maisie stuck her nose out. "Jack! It's so good to see you! Are you hurt? Can you jump up?"

"I'm not hurt, I just couldn't get through the grill on my own, let me try again," said Jack and he jumped up. This time, with Maisie holding the grill open, it was easy and Jack quickly found himself up in the pantry. Then the two dogs squeezed through to the den to join the others.

Back in HQ the small dogs were overjoyed to see Jack back safe and sound. He was sniffed and inspected by each of them, tails wagging as they greeted each other.

Norris was apologetic. "Sorry Jack, I tried to get back for you, but we all got trapped in the den when a box was pushed in front of the entrance. Tell us what happened."

So Jack sat down and recounted the tale of how, once Norris had left him, he'd looked for water and been double crossed by Max who had led the Bigs to him. He told them of the pseudo court they'd held with the cats and the Cairns, of how he'd been frightened but resolute in protecting his friends. Finally, and he hung his head at this point, he told them how he'd named Max as the cats were closing in to hurt him again and this had made them leave him alone, just putting him in solitary confinement for a night. Finally, he told them about Max's cruel words, taunting him about the monsters.

George bristled at the mention of Max taunting Jack. "Looks like Max got his come-uppance, the Bigs caught up with him, can't say I've much sympathy." He looked meaningfully at Maisie. "He's been fooling us all for far too long."

Jack was wide-eyed. "Oh no! I never meant for that to happen, I was just so scared of the cats."

Elsie saw Jack was worried and, smiling to herself at his soft heart, she smoothly intervened. "There's no harm done, Jack. The Bigs gave him a bit of a savaging but the human intervened and all the dogs have been locked up separately in the cages. I think that'll be the end of it now."

Jack was doubtful, but accepted Elsie's words and said nothing more. As the other dogs settled down, he spotted something in the corner behind Norris. "Sock toy!" he exclaimed as he pounced on it then spent a happy while tussling with Norris, all cares forgotten for the moment. The small dogs were thus distracted and laughed at his antics as he and Norris tugged and played with the sock until they were tired. Then all of them settled down in the den and fell into a deep sleep, comforted that they were all safe together for now.

Chapter Fifteen

The telephone rang. Its piercing shrill broke the quiet of the sleeping house. It was still dark outside, dawn was close but had not yet broken. Ring, ring. Ring, ring. There were the sounds of the human hurriedly getting out of bed upstairs, the click of the switch to the light on the landing, then heavy footsteps down the stairs and into the living room. "Hello!" Her greeting as she picked up the receiver, then muffled, anxious conversation. "Right, I'll come now." A click as the handset was replaced.

The small dogs sat under the stairs, keeping very quiet as the human rapidly retraced her steps upstairs and spent a few minutes getting ready before coming down again. She briefly stopped in the hall to put on her coat and then she picked up her old, tattered bag and left the house, shutting the front door behind her with a slam and stepping out into the greyness of the new day.

The house returned to silence. The dogs were still and quiet in their cages, the cats remained hidden under the bed and the small dogs stayed in their den. All stayed quiet as dawn broke and the new day started.

The hours drifted by and there was no return of the human. The cats got bored first and slipped downstairs to the kitchen where they sniffed suspiciously at the remnants of dried up cat food in the dishes and then, deciding they could get better fare elsewhere, left the house via the conservatory, silently passing the cages of locked-up dogs.

The dark shadows of the cats passing the hall den were noticed by Norris who was on guard duty. He was beginning to get bored too. "I'm hungry," he stated as he stood up and stretched.

"Yes, and I'm thirsty too. Can't we go and find some supplies, even the cats have gone past?"

The small dogs looked at Elsie, they trusted her wise judgement and treated her as their leader. "I suppose so," she mused, "the other dogs still seem to be locked up and the cats will have gone out. I think it's a good time to see what's going on out there. Be careful everyone and meet back here."

The dogs filed out of the den, one by one. Now that Toby had moved the box it was easier to scramble out and so, they stepped carefully through the gap and walked out into the hall. They stopped to peer into the living room, but it was deserted, no dogs in there. They passed the door to the dining room, it was slightly ajar and they could see rows of cages, all crammed with dogs. The small troupe slipped by, making no noise, and entered the kitchen relieved to see the large water bowl over by the wall was nearly full. They all took a deep drink each and then relieved themselves back on the hall carpet. There were no rules on toileting in the dog hoarder's house, they simply added to the stinking mess.

There was no food in the kitchen. In her hurry to leave, the human had forgotten to put any food out. The small dogs searched all over the room but, apart from some cat crunchies that Jack's long tongue winkled out, there was nothing.

The dogs in the cages were getting restless too. It had been a long and uncomfortable night, crowded into cramped cages, alongside little known companions and with no room to stretch and scratch. Now the dogs were getting hungry and thirsty too and tempers were starting to fray. A small Yorkshire Terrier snapped at her companion for treading on her paw and this started a wave of snarling and barking from the other dogs.

Toby and Max, crammed into a cage together, regarded each other with suspicion. Max licked at his sore paw and tried to avoid leaning on any of his bite wounds. Fortunately they had been caged right next to the door, at the other end of the row from any Bigs. There was no cage directly above them and the Cairns were up on the row above somewhere, but not near. In the cage next door was old Rogue, still telling his stories of glorious fights to a deaf spaniel who was managing to snooze through them. This gave them both a degree of privacy.

Toby had been trying to get some sleep all night. At first he'd been unhappy at being locked up with Max, remembering vividly Max's cruelty when he'd warned of monsters as the Cairns had taken Toby away to put him into solitary confinement. Elsie had told him about Max's conversation with Maisie where he'd admitted to saying the cruel words and how he'd laughed at their effect and the terror he'd caused. He'd heard that Max had informed on Jack and helped the Bigs to catch and try him. No, Toby was not happy to be placed in a cage with Max and so he turned his back on him and pretended to sleep.

As the night wore on, he could hear Max shifting uneasily behind him, variously licking his paw, then the wounds on his body, and then whimpering as he moved and caught another sore spot. *Good! That'll teach him!* But as time passed, Toby's friendly and helpful nature reasserted itself and he turned around to study his companion who was trying to soothe a sore spot behind his ear but kept catching it with his claw.

"Here, let me help," Toby moved over and started to lick the wound behind Max's ear with his soft tongue. Max lowered his head and stopped whimpering as the warm licking soothed his sore ear. Toby continued with the licking, finding Max's other wounds and gently soothing them with his warm, rhythmic licking. Max lay down and let Toby sort out his wounds until they were all done and no longer quite so sore.

When he finished, Toby sat back and looked piercingly at Max. "That was some mauling the Bigs gave you Max."

"Yeah, I know. They got me good and proper," said Max looking sheepishly at Toby. "Thank you for helping me, I know I don't deserve it."

Toby studied Max, "Why did you do it, Max? You must know you've hurt other dogs, why did you do all those things?"

Max shrugged, "Oh you know, I thought it was fun to tease you and you've got to admit it was a bit ridiculous." He saw Toby's stare harden and added, "I wanted the Bigs to like me and I thought it might impress at least one of the girls." Max looked down at his torn fur and deep, oozing wounds and said, pathetically, "But look at me. The Bigs did this to me and the girls won't look at me now."

Toby sensibly held his tongue since he thought a bit of self reflection in this vein might actually be useful. Instead, he recommended that Max get some rest and try to let his wounds heal. They both curled up as best they could in the cramped cage and snoozed until the grey dawn brought some light into the room and the dogs started to stir.

The dogs had heard the telephone ring and the sound of the human getting ready then leaving the house. There was nothing they could do but they started to get restless and, as the hours passed, and they got hungrier and thirstier, the grumblings started. At first the dogs whimpered and growled softly, but as time went on, it got more urgent and one or two dogs started to bark and howl and more dogs joined in. The noise grew in volume. "Help us, we're trapped and starving!" they shouted. But nobody came.

The small dogs sat in the kitchen den and heard the grumblings starting to get louder and more urgent. They were hungry themselves and it was now past both breakfast and evening meal times yet there was still no sign of the human returning.

Jack's stomach growled with hunger and he watched the cats sneak past the den. They were returning from their outdoor hunting expedition, raindrops glistening on their coats but, finding no food in the kitchen, slunk upstairs to their lair. *Must be raining outside,* he thought, keeping low and quiet as they went past.

Elsie broached the subject first. "I think we're going to have to do something. We're hungry and the caged dogs are hungry and thirsty."

The small dogs nodded hesitantly. They were certainly hungry and wanted to find some food. George spoke up first, "We can send Jack and Maisie into the pantry to get food for us, that'll fill us up." The small dogs brightened at this thought.

Elsie was thoughtful. "Yes, of course we can, but it won't help the other dogs who are locked up. They are both hungry and thirsty."

Norris, who was feeling very hungry himself, couldn't see the problem. "We can't help them, they're locked up. They'll just have to wait for the human. Let's go and get our food now."

The small dogs looked at Elsie. She could see they were hungry and so decided to let them eat, *they could come back to the other dogs later, this was going to be a long night.* "OK, let's go eat!" She led the way out of the kitchen and back to HQ under the stairs. As they passed the dining room the sounds of the other dogs got louder and more desperate. "Help! Help us somebody please!"

The small dogs resolutely carried on to HQ, but Maisie had recognised Toby's voice. *It isn't his fault,* she thought and silently vowed to get him some food.

Once in HQ the small dogs worked efficiently. Maisie and Jack popped through the small gap to the pantry and handed back biscuits and pouches to the dogs waiting on the other side. Maisie passed through a few extra, *for Toby*. Job done, they scrambled back through and ate a hearty supper back in HQ.

Maisie waited until the small dogs had fallen asleep after their meal, then she picked up a pouch and silently left the den. She carried it down to the dining room then pushed at the door until it opened a bit more, just enough for a small dog with a tasty morsel in her mouth to slip through.

The room was dark and the dogs restless but she immediately saw Toby, snoozing in the cage closest to the door but with his back to her. She breathed a faint sight of relief and crept up to the cage, ready to slip the pouch through the bars and back away. By keeping close to the wall and aiming for the side where she couldn't be seen by the occupants of the other cages, she managed to reach the cage without notice. She was just about to push the pouch in, when a head was raised in the cage and she found herself looking straight into the eyes of Max.

Maisie froze. *Max! Max the informer!* But Max stayed quiet, just watching her. Maisie gathered up her last scrap of courage and dropped the pouch in the cage behind Toby and turned away to flee.

"Wait, Maisie." The words were softly spoken. "Please, Maisie, I'm s... I'm sorry." She turned back to see Max's mournful face, his eyes still watching her. She could hardly believe it, *Max was apologising to her!*

Maisie was direct. "What do you want, Max? I only brought some food for Toby. But I'm sure you'll eat that now, you always look after yourself first."

The eyes watched her, Max's gaze steady. "I know you're angry Maisie, and you've every right to be so. But I am sorry and I won't eat Toby's food." His voice took on an urgency, "We're trapped here and we're hungry and thirsty. You can help us."

"Hmph! Why should I help you? Seems to me you've got what you deserved." Maisie was indignant, but even as she spoke she saw that one of Max's eyes was half closed and there was a nasty looking wound above it. His glossy fur was shredded and chunks of it on his ear had been torn out. Her hardened heart melted somewhat but she simply said, "I'll have to see," and she turned once more and slipped quietly out of the dining room and back to HQ before she was missed.

Max sat and watched her depart. He looked down at the pouch and the sleeping body of his new friend. He was sorely tempted to eat it and deny all knowledge of his pledge to Maisie. But he looked down at his sore paw and remembered the kindness of Toby and so he made his decision. "Toby, wake up, look what you've got," he said as he nudged Toby awake.

"W...what's up?" Toby was bleary eyed from his sleep, but he soon woke up fully when he saw the pouch of cat food. "How did that get there?"

"Present, it's a present from Maisie," Max answered, keeping his eyes on the pouch. "She said it was for you, Toby."

Toby was delighted with his present and picked it up and chewed it open. He gulped down half the contents and would have finished it, but his naturally friendly nature made him offer it to Max. With a shake of his golden head he held out the pouch in his teeth. "Go on, Max, we're both hungry, I can't eat it all in front of you." Max gladly took it and devoured the contents.

When Max had finished, Toby looked quizzically at him. "That's a bit better, but I'm still thirsty and we're all still locked up, what did Maisie say?"

"Not much really." Max's brow was furrowed. "I apologised to her, but I don't think she believed me. I asked her to get help for the dogs and she dropped the pouch and left. I don't think we'll get any help from her now and I can't really blame her."

Toby kept his thoughts to himself. He knew how hurt Maisie had been by Max's cavalier behaviour and how Max's actions had harmed his friends, but he was starting to see another side to Max, a side that considered the impact his actions had on others. He decided it would be good for Max to dwell on that a while longer. So he settled down and listened to the periodic grumblings of the locked up dogs. They were hungrier and thirstier now, so it was not as loud or as intense, but that was not a good sign.

Chapter Sixteen

Maisie had crept back into the den and taken her place with the sleeping dogs. She thought that she hadn't been missed and decided to go to sleep and forget all about the locked up dogs. Lying down she closed her eyes, but images of caged dogs haunted her dreams. She turned over and tried again. She saw visions of starving dogs, holding out their paws to her from behind caged bars and pulling at her, calling her to help them. She started in her sleep, briefly woke up and turned over again.

A voice close to her whispered, "Are you alright, Maisie? Can't you sleep?" She opened her eyes to see a concerned George watching her.

"Oh George, no I can't sleep. I keep seeing those dogs, all locked up and starving and calling for help..." Maisie paused, looked intently at George and realised she could trust this gruff but faithful dog and made a decision to come clean. "I w..., I went to see Toby. I wanted to give him some food so I kept an extra food pouch and took it to him. He's in the cage at the end so I slipped in without the other dogs knowing and went up to him."

This much George had guessed. He'd seen Maisie take the extra food and had made sure she thought he was asleep like the others. Then he had seen her go and return and witnessed her tossing and turning as she tried to block out her thoughts and get to sleep. He simply said, "Go on."

"Oh George, it was horrid. Toby was sleeping so I tried to drop the pouch in the cage, but Max was there! Max was there in the cage with Toby and he was watching me!"

George sensed her distress. "What did you do?"

Maisie looked down at her paws. "Well he spoke to me. He said he was sorry which I didn't believe, but…"

"It's OK, go on."

"But I saw what they'd done to him, those horrible, horrible Bigs. They'd beaten him, bitten and wounded him. Oh George, he's a real mess."

"Well I think he had it coming, don't you?" George wasn't overly sympathetic with his rival.

"A little, perhaps," accepted Maisie, "but he seemed… he seemed changed somehow. Max said he wouldn't eat Toby's food but he asked me to help all the dogs. They were hungry and thirsty, he said. He asked me to get help."

George was thoughtful. He could tell Maisie had told him the whole story and he was quietly proud of her kindness and her giving nature. Yet he was worried for her, Max was not to be trusted, he'd shown that. But George knew that what he said about the dogs being hungry and thirsty would be true. There was still no sign of the human, it was time to act. "I think he's right and we have to do something. Let's wake the others and see what they think."

So the small dogs were roused from their slumber and Maisie told them her story again. They argued to and fro for a while as they worked through their anger at how Jack had been treated, but eventually came to the same conclusion, they had to help.

"Right," said Elsie, taking the lead once more. "We need a plan. We know we can get food, but it's slow progress and then what about water?."

The dogs discussed various ideas but they were all a bit slow and difficult, it was a pity they didn't have better access to the garage.

"That's it," chimed in Jack. He waved a paw in the air, "We need to get into the garage from the kitchen. Then we have access to the cats' water bowl as well as the dogs' one in the kitchen and we could even try filling bottles again. We could get Maisie to throw the food out of the grill into the garage and it would be much faster doing that than squeezing the food via HQ. We just need to open the door from the kitchen to the garage."

"Good plan, Jack," agreed Elsie, "but how do we open that door?"

"I dunno exactly, but the Cairns managed it when they put me in solitary. I think they reached up and did something to the handle thing." Jack was eager, a small problem like a closed door wasn't going to stop him. "We need Toby, Toby will know how to open it." Then a final thought occurred to him, "And Toby can reach!"

And so it was agreed, they would open the door to the garage and get food and water for the dogs that way. But first, they needed to free Toby.

One by one the small dogs crept out of the den. The day had passed by as they made their deliberations and plans, now it had gone dark. There was just enough street light filtering in through the glass panel in the front door to light their way as they moved steadily down the hall and pushed open the door to the dining room.

The room was dark and quiet, but as they entered the room, the low level grumbling started up again. "Help, help us please!"

Elsie walked around the cages and stood in front, letting her eyes adjust. She was shocked. The room was warm and the smell was awful, worse than normal in the dog hoarder house because the dogs had urinated and defaecated in their cages. They were so crammed in they had no choice but to lie in it, they sat and lay as best they could with their eyes half closed and tongues hanging out. Some dogs had tried chewing at the cage bars in a desperate attempt to get out and had bleeding gums and sore teeth.

Toby recognised her first and shouted out, "Elsie! Elsie, it's Toby! Over here!" but Elsie stood a while longer, carefully surveying the cages. She noticed the Bigs over towards the far wall, watching her carefully, and the Cairns up on the second row, crammed in together and also studying her. *They would need to take care,* she noted.

One at a time, the other small dogs joined her, wrinkling their noses at the stench, watching the cages in dismay.

Norris stated the obvious, "Stinks in here!" but the rest of the small dogs stayed silent.

"Right, let's get to work, we need to free Toby." Elsie approached the end cage where Toby was waiting, and touched noses with him through the cage bars. "Hi Toby, we need your help, we're going to try to free you first." Then she saw the dark shape of another dog standing behind Toby and, remembering Maisie's story, hissed, "Who's that? Who's in there with you? Is that you, Max?"

Max came forward in the cage and Elsie saw his half closed eye and shredded fur. "Yes Elsie, I'm here too. I won't cause you any trouble, just help us all please."

"We'll see about that, but I'll take your word for now." Elsie was slightly dubious but she had no choice really, they needed to free Toby and Max was in the same cage. "Do you promise to help us?"

"Yes I promise."

"Okay, then let's start." Elsie signalled to Jack to approach the cage. "Jack here has a knack of undoing things and escaping, so he's going to try first, stand back."

Jack came forward as the larger dogs moved back from the cage door. He stood up on his back legs and reached his mouth up to the door catch. It was a long metal bolt which had a lever which must be lifted and then slid back to release it. Jack studied it carefully for a moment then used his long tongue to ease under and to grab and lift the metal lever. It took him a couple of attempts to get a good grip but gradually he managed to pull it and slide the bolt over. The door was unlocked. "There, that's done it, give it a push, Toby," he said and stood back as Toby pushed at the bars and the door swung open.

Toby stepped out of the cage first, followed by Max. Both dogs stretched, glad to get out of the cramped confines of the cage, Max a little more stiffly as his wounds were hurting. The small dogs gathered round and sniffed them, they were all shocked at the sight of Max's wounds.

Even George was startled as he gruffly acknowledged Max. "They worked you over good and proper, didn't they?" Max nodded glumly.

The dogs in the other cages were watching. "Help us, free us next," they pleaded.

But Elsie shook her head, they had a plan and they were safer with the other dogs secured. "Come on Toby, we need your help in the kitchen," she said then she turned and led the way out of the dining room as the cacophony of noise rose behind them. Max shrugged and followed, he'd made his choice, he was one of them now.

Once they reached the kitchen they stopped to let Toby and Max take a long drink at the water bowl. They were thirsty and lapped for some minutes until the water there grew low. *Water's going to be a priority,* thought Elsie as she waited for them to finish.

When they were finished she motioned to Jack to step forward, this part of the plan was his idea after all. Jack pointed at the door to the garage and said, "Toby, we need to get into the garage, and we need to open that door. Do you remember when the Cairns put you in solitary confinement? Did you see how they opened the door?"

Toby put his golden head on one side, thinking hard, "I can't really remember it exactly. Because of being so terrified you see." He cast a disapproving look at Max. "On account of monsters you know," he added. He took a quiet pleasure in seeing Max wince, but nevertheless, he looked hard at the door. "I think one of them reached up and grabbed that metal thing and pulled it open," he said, squinting at the door and pointing at the door handle. "Tell you what, I'll try it myself now."

Toby went up to the door and stood up on his hind legs and put his mouth round the door handle and pulled. The small dogs clustered round, giving him encouragement but the door stayed closed. Toby stopped pulling for a moment then tried again, pulling with all his might, his paws scrabbling for purchase on the tiled floor. The door stayed stubbornly shut.

The small dogs were disappointed, their plan hadn't worked and they sat and looked despondently at the firmly shut door.

A voice piped up from the doorway to the kitchen, "Can I help?" It was Max, he had watched Toby's failed efforts at opening the door with increasing frustration. "I saw the Cairns open the door and I think I know how it's done."

Elsie turned to look at him. "OK Max, how's it done?"

"You have to turn the metal thing down somehow, do you want me to try?" As she nodded, Max stepped forward and Toby moved away to give him space. Max reached up and grabbed the end of the handle with his teeth and pulled it down. The latch released with a loud click and as he pulled, the door started to move. Toby quickly put a paw through the small gap between the door and the frame and together the dogs pulled and pushed the door open.

The sound of rain on the garage roof grew louder as the door swung open and Toby smiled as he remembered. "So that's your plan, Jack. Same as before?" he said as he stepped down into the garage.

Max was confused. "What plan?" he asked.

Jack carefully told him about his plan to collect rainwater dripping into the garage to refill the water bowls and to give to the locked-up thirsty dogs. He explained that they all would need to find plastic bottles and cups and containers in the house and garage and that Toby would be in charge of filling them up.

"Excellent idea," piped up George who'd been listening carefully and he immediately set to work organising the dogs. He gave them their first work tasks. Jack, Norris and Maisie could collect containers from the house, Max and Elsie would look for some more in the garage and he and Toby himself would manage the filling up of bottles and water bowls. Once they had enough water collected they would start the distribution.

And so the dogs worked together. Under George's watchful eye, they made a slick production line, finding and delivering containers from the house and garage to be filled and sorted and lined up waiting for delivery. The small pile of bottles and cups gradually grew in size until George indicated that they should be used to fill the water bowls in the garage and kitchen. These were for the workers to lap at, after all it was busy, thirsty work.

For a while the rain drummed down heavily on the garage roof and the drips came fast and furious, down the walls and through breaks in the roofing. The dogs hurried to place containers under the drips and to replace them when full. But as the night wore on the rain slowed and then stopped and the drips dried up. Nevertheless, the dogs had made an impressive mountain of containers, all filled with the rainwater.

Chapter Seventeen

Elsie surveyed the dogs' handiwork and was well pleased. "Good work everyone, we've collected plenty of water. Now we need to get it to the caged dogs. Anyone got any ideas on how we do this?"

Jack piped up, "We should be able to use the bottles and the small cups to offer the water to the dogs on the bottom row. It might work for the ones on top of them too, if we use Toby and Max to stretch up, but there are two cages on top of those with small dogs in them and I don't think we can reach those."

Elsie was practical as ever. "We'll just have to think of something for them later, best start getting the water delivered to the others now. Small dogs, you can water the bottom row, Max and Toby the middle."

And so they started to deliver water to the caged dogs. Firstly, George and Norris dragged cups and bowls and placed them on the floor in front of the lower cages. The dogs inside stretched their tongues out through the cage bars to lap at the water. Jack, Maisie and Elsie formed a small supply chain, fetching bottles and topping up the containers as they were emptied and moved on to the next cage,

Old Rogue was the first to get some water. The old warrior lapped it up, and, stump of a tail wagging, he thanked the small dogs. His companion, the deaf spaniel, was next and had to be nudged towards the water, but he too drank thankfully. The dogs worked their way down the row and Max and Toby followed, offering bowls and cups of water in their mouths to dogs up on the row above who gratefully drank from them. They reached the Cairns and wondered if there'd be trouble, but Sue and Stu simply accepted the water offered with no comment and the dogs moved on.

They worked as a team, moving and refilling bowls and cups until they reached the cages with the Bigs inside. These were bigger cages which protruded further forward and there were two rows of cages on top of them which were difficult to get to. In the first cage was Titan, glaring at the small dogs and showing his gleaming teeth. George eyed him warily and called a halt.

"What's up small dog, aren't you going to give me any water?" growled Titan. He pressed his face up close to the cage door. "Wait till I get out, you'll regret it then, you and your friends." He glared meaningfully at Max who shrank back, his wounds still smarting from the last encounter.

The small dogs had a problem. They needed access to the cages above but they would need to stand on top of the cages occupied by the Bigs to reach them. None of them fancied having their legs snapped at by those enormous jaws, they were going to have to strike a bargain of some kind.

But how to negotiate with terrorists?

George looked past Titan's cage, in the next cage was Ruby and then Sidney in the very corner. The two other Bigs both sat watching the small dogs, waiting for their next move. From the cages above, the now familiar wails started up again. "Help us, help us, we're thirsty too." He knew they had to act.

He turned first to Ruby. "Hi Ruby, we don't want any trouble but we need to get water to all the dogs. We can only reach the ones above you if we climb on your cage. If you allow us to do that, we can bring you water too."

Ruby felt Sidney's eyes on her, watching her carefully, and could hear the low grumbles in Titan's throat, warning her not to change sides. But she was hungry and very, very thirsty. She was also getting tired of threatening the small dogs. Normally placid and lazy by nature, she had got caught up in the plans by the other Bigs when they had pushed her to help them. She looked at Max and saw his wounds and made up her mind. "Yes, I'll help you. But you must give water to Sidney and Titan too."

And so the deal was made. The small dogs searched around and found a footstool. It had raggedy edges but when they pushed it in front of Ruby's cage, it provided enough of a step for Toby to climb up and stand teetering on the top edge of Ruby's cage. Norris stood on the stool next and passed up the cups and bowls of water which Toby held out to the caged dogs on the middle row.

There were two more cages stacked on the very top and Toby tentatively reached up and offered water to the dogs in the nearest one. The farthest one, though, was in the corner, above the cage that Sidney still prowled in. Its occupant, a little Yorkshire terrier named Betsy, looked out with pleading eyes. She called out to Toby, "Don't forget me, I'm thirsty too." But Toby couldn't reach her unless he stood on Sidney's cage and Sidney had no intention of making that easy for him. Sidney growled and snapped at his paws whenever they came close and even the disapproving looks of Ruby didn't stop him. Toby gave up and hopped down to the ground, they needed another plan for this last cage.

The small dogs sat staring at the tower of cages, trying to think of another way to get water up to the last cage. How could they pass anything to Betsy with Sidney there? Could they negotiate with Sidney? Could they distract him?

As they mulled it over, Jack was struck by a thought. "Could we use... perhaps we could..." he said mysteriously then, as the others turned to look at him, he ran out of the room at high speed in the direction of HQ.

Norris shrugged. "One of his mad turns I expect." He wasn't at all surprised when, a minute later, Jack returned with his sock. A bit bored of being helpful and always up for some fun, Norris sprang forward for a game.

"No, no, no!" Jack cried, "It's not for you, it's for Betsy!"

"I'm not sure Betsy's in a position to play sock with you, she has more pressing needs," chimed in George, a bit confused.

"That's what I've brought sock for! We can soak it in the water and pass it through the cages to her."

"Goodness! Yes it might just work, great idea Jack." Elsie approved.

So Jack soaked his sock in the water and the dogs passed it carefully up to Betsy, weaving it between the cage bars and passing it via the caged dogs to reach her. She took it thankfully and squeezed it hard, drinking the water that dripped out. "More please," she requested as she sent the sock back. Jack's plan was working, three more times of passing the sock and she was full. "Thank you!" she shouted down.

Sidney glowered in his cage below, glaring through the bars at Jack and his sock. "I told you, no play things, small dog. You and your friends will pay for this."

Jack quivered, he was frightened. He saw the threat in Sidney's eyes and he hadn't forgotten the time that the Bigs had turned on him in the kitchen and the bite marks he'd seen on Max. He was glad Sidney was behind bars for now, but how long would that last? He closed his eyes for a moment, then gathered up all his courage to reply. "We are helping the dogs, we are giving them water and when we have done that we will help you too. Your threats are pointless, they help nobody." The tiny dog stood as tall and proud as his small body allowed and added, "*We* work together and help *all* the dogs."

"Hmph!" replied Sidney, carefully eyeing the small, snappy dog and remembering that he himself was very thirsty. "You help all the dogs you say? Well, where's my water?"

"Yeah, where's our water, small dog? Give it to us now!" Titan joined in, his face pressed against the cage front.

Jack flinched a little but stood his ground. He knew the Bigs were behind bars and couldn't hurt him. *He would make them wait.*

"They're thirsty too, Jack," a soft voice whispered in his ear. He turned to see Maisie who had come up behind him, holding a small bowl of water. "We should give them water next, they've waited long enough."

He knew she was right. The tiniest of all the dogs, who had the smallest paws and the biggest heart, was absolutely right. "You're right, let's give them the water." Jack took the bowl from her and walked up to Sidney, putting it down in front of him and waiting whilst the big dog lapped at the water through the bars.

This was the signal for the other dogs to move into action and they brought water to Titan and Ruby too. Elsie held Ruby's bowl out to her and she gratefully drank while Max pushed a cup carefully towards Titan and stepped back quickly as he lunged aggressively towards it, spilling most of it but lapping up what he could.

The rest of the small dogs kept up the water supply chain as before, refilling the containers as they emptied, keeping a careful distance from the big dogs. Soon the Bigs were finished.

The room had grown quiet whilst the water was being given out but now another low grumble started. "Feed us, we're hungry. Feed us now."

Chapter Eighteen

The small dogs withdrew to the kitchen for a pow-wow. Max and Toby, hearing the grumbling dogs in the cages, looked at each other and followed. They were all tired and thirsty, but after another lap at the water bowl, they started to organise themselves once more.

The difficulty was that they didn't want to give away any more of their secrets to Max, but they really needed his help. Elsie looked searchingly at Max, "Max, we need your help on this. Remember your promise?" Max nodded and, satisfied for now, she started to outline the plan to them all.

Jack and Maisie would enter the pantry via HQ and start to pass out as much food as they could through the grill into the garage. The bigger dogs, Max and Toby, would take turns to stretch over the box below the grill to receive the food, Toby could show Max just where to go. Norris, George and herself would shuttle the food into the kitchen where they would pile it up until they had enough to distribute.

The dogs agreed and hurried away to get started on their part of the plan. It took a little while for Jack and Maisie to squeeze through to the pantry and get into position, but soon all sorts of food was being passed out through the grill. Cat food pouches, dog biscuits, dry dog and cat food by the mouthful, all were carefully passed between the dogs and carried into the kitchen where a pile started to mount up.

Jack and Maisie worked tirelessly in the pantry, chewing open packaging to get at the food, then passing it between themselves to create a pile by the grill. Maisie took up position at the grill first as she was quite good at holding the grill open with one paw whilst grabbing the food with her mouth and pushing it out with the other paw.

Toby and Max got into position on the garage side with Max closest to the grill, standing in the box below, jaws ready to receive the food and Toby standing a little bit back. Max looked up at Maisie as she passed a pouch of cat food to him. "I really am sorry you know." He put the pouch down carefully beside the box on the garage floor.

Maisie ignored him and poked a large dog biscuit toward him. It dropped into the box he was standing in.

He searched the box, retrieved the biscuit from amongst the pine cones and tried again. "I wanted to thank you."

Clang! Another biscuit dropped into the box. "Thank me? Whatever for?" Maisie's face was expressionless.

Max dutifully fetched out the biscuit and passed it to Toby, along with the other one. "For coming back and helping. For trusting me again."

Maisie was angry. "Trust! You don't know the meaning of the word," she snarled and thrust another biscuit out, then another. "You betrayed my friends, you betrayed us all." And for good measure she spat out a mouthful of cat crunchies at him.

"Whoa, Maisie, not so fast!" He scrabbled around in the box, trying to pick up the biscuits. "I'm still sorry I hurt you and your friends, I promise I won't do it again. Please don't give me a hard time, I'm trying to help."

"We'll see. I don't know why it matters to you." She spat another mouthful of cat crunchies at him and pushed out a pouch which dropped into the box.

"Well, for a start, could we get a better system going here?" He rummaged around the box, trying to find all the dropped food.

"Better system?" Her voice was high and brittle sounding.

Max put his head on one side and looked her straight in the eye. "I could help here," he said softly. "Please, Maisie, let's work together."

Maisie wasn't immune to his charm. "Huh! Well what do you propose then?"

"Let me hold the grill open for you, then you can pass the food directly to Toby and we won't drop any. We can work quicker that way."

She knew he was right and anyway her anger was evaporating. She didn't like to hold grudges and his help would make her job easier. She nodded. "Alright, let's give it a try."

So Max called Toby closer and moved forward to take hold of the grill. Maisie could now work faster and with more accuracy, passing the food directly out to Toby who put the items straight onto the floor beside the box for the small dogs to collect and take for the ever growing pile in the kitchen.

They worked well as a team and within quite a short space of time they received the message back from Elsie. "Enough! We have enough, come back to the kitchen."

Jack heard the news and nudged Maisie from behind. "Come on then, let's go join the others!" He motioned with his paw that she should jump down through the grill, into the garage.

Maisie was dubious. The garage was dark and gloomy and it seemed a long way down into the box filled with pine cones and who-knows-what. "I'm not sure, Jack. Can't we go back through the house instead?"

"We could, but it's two squeezes instead of one. What are you frightened of?"

Maisie shrugged, she wasn't sure herself. Perhaps she still didn't trust Max who stood in the box, up to his shoulders in pine cones.

"It's okay Maisie, it's safe to jump here," Max said and he cleared a small space in the pine cones for her to jump into.

Maisie decided to be very brave, closed her eyes and jumped. She landed safely in the box then scrambled out, over the edge, and onto the garage floor.

"Good girl!" Max was impressed. "Now it's your turn, Jack."

Jack didn't need any further encouragement and he followed Maisie, jumping down into the box, then over the side and onto the garage floor. All the dogs then crossed the garage and jumped up the step into the kitchen.

As before with the water, the small dogs organised themselves and, with the help of Max and Toby, set up a way of distributing the food to the caged dogs. This time, the Bigs raised no objections to the feeding of dogs above them. Betsy was passed a small pouch of food and some dog biscuits and then food was pushed into the cages of the Bigs. The cries of "help us" and "we're hungry" slowly diminished until every dog was fed and the dining room fell silent.

Elsie surveyed the cages, looking to see if any dog was still in need, but there was just the sound of contented chewing and Titan occasionally uttering a low growl if anyone passed his cage, which she ignored. "There, that's everyone fed for now." She yawned, "I think it's time for some sleep. Max and Toby, I'm going to leave you two here, on guard. Just bark if you need us."

Indeed they were all very sleepy after their night's work, so no further persuasion was needed. The small dogs filed out of the dining room, quietly so as not to disturb the caged dogs, and went into the living room where it was quieter and the air was cleaner. There, they jumped onto the settee and comfy chair and, within a very few moments, fell fast asleep.

All the dogs were still deep in sleep when there was a loud knocking at the front door.

Chapter Nineteen

"Rat-a-tat-tat!" Someone was knocking in the door. "Rat-a-tat-tat." There it was again.

Jack woke up with a start. "Woof" he shouted, "woof woof!"

"Hello! Is anyone in there?" A human voice shouted through the letterbox.

"Woof woof!" Jack shouted back as he jumped off the comfy chair and ran into the hall, closely followed by the other small dogs who took up the barking chorus as they ran. "Woof woof, we're in here!" they barked.

"Hello! Mrs Rogers? Are you there Mrs Rogers?" the voice shouted again, louder this time, trying to be heard above the barking.

"Woof woof woof! We're here, please help us," chorused the dogs.

"She isn't answering the door, what do we do next?" The human spoke to her companion, the dogs couldn't hear the response.

Now the caged dogs had heard the voices and they added to the commotion. "Woof woof! Please help us!" they shouted as loud as they could. Max and Toby, roused from their slumber, joined in the barking but stayed on guard in the dining room, just as instructed by Elsie.

"Goodness, it sounds like there's rather a lot of them." The voice sounded worried, "Perhaps we'd better take a look around?"

"Sshhh! Quiet a moment!" Jack shushed the dogs and listened intently.

There was the sound of the humans walking around the house and rattling door handles and trying to look in the filthy windows. They stopped outside the conservatory at the back of the house and peered through the dirty, broken glass panes. "Mrs Rogers? Are you in there?"

This caused an even louder outbreak of barking from the rows of caged dogs in the house.

"What do you think you're doing?" Another, familiar voice asked. At the sound of this new voice, the sound from the dogs grew louder still as they recognised her and so the exchange of words between all of the humans couldn't be heard. Nevertheless, within a few moments the first set of visitors had gone back round to the front of the house and were standing at the front door, waiting as Mrs Rogers fumbled in her handbag for her house keys.

As the door opened and the humans entered the house the small dogs rushed towards them, barking loudly. "Help us! Help us please!" they shouted. "We're starving!"

"Yes, yes my lovelies," said their human as she patted the jumping dogs, "now quieten down for me." She led the way into the living room, followed excitedly by the small dogs, and motioned for the visitors to sit down on the settee. Maisie recognised the ample rear end of one of the visitors, who looked suspiciously at the settee before she sat down. The other visitor they didn't recognise, a tall blond lady, dressed in black trousers and a white blouse, who looked quickly round the room and sat down next to the fat lady.

It was a little time before the small dogs settled. They pushed their noses into the hands of the visitors and jumped on the settee, pawing at arms and wagging their tails. Jack shyly gave them a quick sniff and wag of his tail then spotted the empty lap of Mrs Rogers who was sitting on the comfy chair. He jumped up onto the chair and nuzzled her until she moved her hands and he could sit on her knee. *Ah bliss!* Jack always felt safe sitting on her knee and he lay down there to watch proceedings. George and Maisie positioned themselves on the settee between the visitors and Norris and Elsie sat down on the floor in front of them. The barking from the next room settled down to a background grumble.

The fat lady broke the silence first. "Now Mrs Rogers, thank you for meeting with us."

The human didn't respond, she sat stroking the small dog on her lap and glared at the visitors.

The fat lady tried again. "Let me introduce my colleague, Sarah Cuthbert. Miss Cuthbert works for our animal control department." She wafted her hand towards the lady sitting beside her.

Again there was no response, the human sat and stared at the wall behind the visitors. She paused her stroking of the small dog which turned and licked her hand, willing her to resume her soft caresses, which she slowly did.

The other visitor spoke. "Mrs Rogers, we've received information about the number of dogs in this house and we would like to investigate. Would it be alright if I ask you a few questions and take a look at the animals?"

The human stopped her stroking completely then and nodded mutely at the visitors.

"Right, let's get started then." Sarah drew out a small notebook and pen from her pocket. "How many dogs do you have in this house, Mrs Rogers? Are they all properly cared for?"

A shrug.

"Right, well I can see 1,2...5 in here." She picked up George who was sitting beside her and looked at him carefully. "Small, long haired, ginger coloured dog," she spoke as she wrote the words down, "tufts of hair missing due to scratching, signs of flea infestation, unneutered, poor condition."

The human sat quietly as Sarah carried on making notes about the small dogs. A sad looking crew they were too. They all sat, scratching at their fleas, ribs thinly covered and with tufts of hair missing and bald patches in their coats. "Wormers?" she queried. "Has a vet seen these dogs?" There was no reply.

Sarah stood up. "Mrs Rogers, we heard other dogs when we came in. I'd like to see those dogs now please."

The human closed her eyes and waved towards the door to the hall.

"Thank you." Sarah moved towards the door, at which point all the small dogs became animated once more and jumped off the seats and followed her. She walked across the hall and pushed the dining room door open.

The smell hit her first and she gagged at the stench. The room was in darkness because the curtains were closed, but small gaps in the curtains allowed a bit of light to penetrate. Two dogs came running up to her, but she didn't recognise the breeds as their stinking fur was so tangled and matted. One had clumps of torn fur hanging off it and many injuries including a half closed eye and she correctly deduced that some of the dogs had been fighting. These two dogs were friendly and wagged their tails at her and followed her round as she took a closer look at the cages piled in rows along one wall.

She noted there were many, many dogs. She counted at least 15 cages all with at least one dog in, most with two. There was no food or water in the cages just some discarded packets and bowls lying in the room. Even from a distance, all of the dogs smelled and looked in poor condition. In the largest cages, some big dogs growled nervously as she inspected them. Shaking her head, the realisation slowly came to her that action would need to be taken swiftly. She walked slowly back to the living room, accompanied closely by the troop of small dogs who had followed her and now filed back into the living room and resumed their positions.

She nodded to the fat lady as she sat down once more and turned to speak to the human. "Mrs Rogers, I've made a cursory inspection and from what I've seen there are upwards of thirty dogs in this house, some in cages and all in poor condition. I would like to call in animal welfare support so we can properly assess the animals and see if they need veterinary treatment."

The human shook her head and started to silently cry. Great big, salty tears rolled down her cheeks and the small dog who had jumped back onto her lap licked her face. The fat lady took pity on her, "Mrs Rogers, we're trying to help you. It's obvious to me the dogs have got a bit much for you, let Sarah here get some help to sort them out. We can work with you."

At last the human spoke, "Not my dogs, not my little dogs! I only went to see my sister, you see. She's not well, she's been in the hospital, I had to go and see her. I didn't want the dogs to fight, you understand. They get a bit naughty and they fight. I had to put them in the cages to stop them. It's not their fault, don't take my dogs!" She sobbed as she spoke and the small white dog licked her tear stricken face once more.

The fat lady leaned forward. "I can see things have been… difficult for you, Mrs Rogers. Let us get some help for you." The human sobbed some more then nodded sadly. Sarah took a mobile phone out of her pocket and walked out into the hall where she made a call and spoke quickly to someone before returning.

The fat lady spoke again, not unsympathetically. "Right Mrs Rogers, things are being organised. I can see it's been a bit of a shock for you, perhaps you should have a cup of tea now. If you'd like I could get that made for you now whilst we wait." Again the human nodded and so the fat lady walked into the kitchen, accompanied by the troop of small dogs, where she rummaged until she found what she needed. She rinsed out a mug and switched the kettle on and gathered together a teabag and some sugar. Looking in the fridge she could tell there was no fresh milk. *Oh well it'll have to do black,* she thought as she put another spoon of sugar in and carried the drink back to the living room, followed closely once more by the small dogs.

Time passed slowly. The hot drink sat untouched on the coffee table and the small dogs took up their positions again. The quiet was only punctuated by the ticking of the clock on the mantelpiece and the occasional whimper from the dogs in the dining room when they thought they'd been forgotten. Humans and dogs sat quietly, waiting.

Part Three - On The Move

Chapter Twenty

The sound of a van drawing up outside the house and doors being slammed broke the silence. The small dogs all jumped up, barking excitedly as the fat lady got to her feet and went to open the front door. Two uniformed figures stood on the doorstep and she invited the man and woman inside.

The new visitors went into the living room where they spoke at length to the human and waved pens and pieces of paper around until, it seemed, things were settled. Then, whilst the fat lady sat quietly comforting the human, the new visitors went back outside and brought in various pieces of equipment such as leads and more cages. Then they paused, the roundup was about to start.

Jack sat still on the human's lap, quivering with fear. The human continued to stroke him as her tears fell and so he stayed there, quiet and still and watched events unfold.

Firstly, the other small dogs were rounded up and put into special cages that had been brought into the hall. Maisie and Elsie were put in one cage and George and Norris in another. A numbered tag was put around their necks and a note of each captured dog written down on a notepad. Toby and Max were captured next, labelled and put back into their cage in the dining room. Finally, the man approached the human and indicated for her to pass Jack to him. Jack shrank further away from him and tried to hide behind the human's hands. The man was having none of it and firmly reached forward and picked Jack up by the scruff of his neck, carried him out into the hall where he was labelled and pushed into a cage perched on top of the others.

Now that all the dogs were secured, the visitors took a careful look around all the rooms in the house, making notes and taking pictures with their mobile phones. "Evidence." Jack heard the man say.

The uniformed humans searched methodically through the house but the cats had made themselves scarce at the first sign of visitors that day, so apart from the dogs in cages in the dining room and the dogs they'd captured that morning, there were no other animals in the house. They went out into the garage and surveyed the piles on the floor, catching their breaths as they smelt the dirt and mess. The man wrenched open the door to the outhouse at the back of the garage, stared briefly in disbelief and then gagged. He called his colleague over and together they stared in horror at the contents..

The dogs in cages in the house heard the commotion, but didn't know the reason for it. The visitors came back through the house past the small dogs in their cages and out to get more things from the van parked outside. When they came back past them, this time they were wearing white coveralls over their uniforms and carrying large, clear plastic bags.

There were sounds of muttered conversations in the garage and things being photographed and noted before being moved and covered. Then slowly, one by one, the bags were filled and carried out through the hall on the way to the waiting van.

As the man passed the dogs in the hall, they caught a glimpse of the contents of the bags. They didn't quite comprehend what they saw at first, the man was carrying dogs, but these were not like any dogs they recognised. These dogs were stiff and still, their flesh shrunken beneath their fur, their eyes dulled and unseeing.

Maisie was shocked and turned away. "Are they... are they dead?" She asked in a whisper.

Elsie nodded sadly as she watched the bags as they were carried respectfully past. She thought she recognised the contents of one, but it was hard to tell if the chocolate fur was indeed Millie, one of Ruby's pups who had disappeared mysteriously some months ago, an act which had contributed to Ruby's hardening heart and alignment with the other Bigs.

The man removed one, two, then three bags from the house, carrying them quickly past the shocked and silent small dogs. He was just carrying the fourth through the hall when a commotion broke out in the dining room. The small dogs jumped as they heard a snarling, snapping sound and the man put the bag he was carrying down on a box in the hall and hurried back to investigate.

The fourth bag was left in full view of the small dogs in the cages in the hall. They could see inside the plastic the curled up figure of a tiny, cream dog. Jack immediately recognised the figure.

George nudged Norris and whispered, "Is that…?"

Norris looked carefully and nodded. He recognised the white, heart shaped patch on the chest. A tiny, valiant dog with a big heart, that was Jack's mum. Or rather, had been. There she was now, lying stiff and still in a bag, on a box in the hall.

The commotion in the dining room had died down and the man returned, picked up the bag and carried it out to his van.

Jack stared after the man, watching the front door long after he'd gone through it and for ages after the slam of the van door and the starting up of the engine had sounded. As the van moved off, Jack let out a long low moan and rocked from side to side.

The small dogs, stuck in cages below him, could do nothing to comfort him and try to ease his grief. They sat quietly in their cages, listening to him shaking and letting out mournful howls as he grieved his loss.

Chapter Twenty One

The van returned to the house and the man and the woman conferred. It seemed that all of the dogs were now suitably caged, labelled and documented and the next phase could commence. "Bitches first for this trip," the woman stated.

The front door to the house was propped open and the humans began to carry cages of dogs out to the van. They started by pulling out the cages with the bigger dogs and loading some of those. Ruby was first, the man and the woman both carrying her cage out past the small dogs, her worried face pressed against the cage door as she disappeared out of the front door. Next was Sue, already split up from Stu and, not so brave now, crying sadly for him. Other cages followed, now with smaller dogs including Betsy, glad to be on the move away from her high perch in the dining room and yapping with excitement.

Finally the man returned to the hall, lifted Jack's cage up and pulled the cage with Elsie and Maisie in it out of the pile. As he swung the cage out of the pile, the two girls scrabbled around to keep their balance and Maisie cried out in panic, "Help, help us!"

George rushed forward to his cage door. "Maisie!" he called and pushed at the door in vain.

Hearing his voice, she turned and called for him. "George! They're taking us away! George...".

Bashing and pushing at the door, George could only shout back at the retreating dogs. "Maisie, don't worry, I'll find you. Be brave!"

And then they were gone. The front door closed, the uniformed figures climbed into the van, slammed the door and started up the engine, then the van roared off down the road carrying its precious cargo away.

The house grew quiet again. The only sound was the soft crying of the human in the living room as the fat lady held her hand and the low moaning of Jack as he sat in his cage and grieved for his mum. Two lost souls mourning their loss. Sarah, shifting uncomfortably as the minutes stretched out, went to the kitchen to make another drink and then dogs and humans waited in silence whilst the tea grew cold once more.

The day wore on and the dogs started to get restless. Titan, still stuck in his cage and with a large red label stuck to his collar, growled threateningly at any dog who looked at him. Rogue was still muttering to himself of the glory days, but quietly, so nobody really took much notice. Jack's moaning had abated and he sat looking at the front door. Sarah went to the front window a few times and twitched the curtain back to look out into the street but there was no sign of the van returning.

Then they heard the dull roar of the engine. It grew louder and louder until the van drew up outside the house and next the engine was switched off, the van doors slammed and Sarah went to the front door to let the uniformed figures into the house once more.

This sparked a lot of barking from the bored dogs and it was a few minutes before she could ask if everything had gone alright to which the man responded yes and that they would "get on with the rest now".

This pronouncement had the effect of prompting more howls and tears from the human and so the fat lady held her hand and soothed her and Sarah offered yet more tea as the uniformed figures of the pet inspectors started their final task.

Titan was first to be moved out. He growled and glared at the other dogs as the man and woman heaved his cage up off the floor and out of the house. Sydney was next, surprisingly sanguine about the experience as the humans laboured under his weight and carried him out. Stu went after him, his eyes still scanning the rooms and hall for Sue as he was ferried out to the van. Next, an assortment of dogs were moved out including old Rogue, blindly fighting his fights still and then Max and Toby, valiantly buoying each other up.

The dining room was empty now and the pet inspectors came into the hall to pick up the final two cages and take their leave. The man picked up the cage with George and Norris in it and swiftly carried it away, but the woman picked up Jack's cage and paused a moment to say goodbye to the other humans.

"That's all of them, we'll be off now, back for the cats later," she shouted as she stood in the doorway to the living room.

The human, on hearing these words and with her hand still held by the fat lady, rose up and staggered forwards. "My dogs, you're taking my dogs!" she cried. She spied Jack in the cage swinging from the woman's hand. "My baby, my poor baby!" she screeched, but Jack closed his eyes and turned his back on her. He could still only see the stiff, frozen figure of his mum and he had no forgiveness to give.

The fat lady made a firmer grab at the human's hand. "Go now!" she cried and gestured at the door with her other hand. The woman heaved up the cage then turned and swiftly walked out of the house, closing the front door with a click behind her. She marched down the path and, meeting the man, deposited Jack's cage into the back of the van and got into the passenger seat. The man quickly scanned his eyes over the cages in the back of the van and, satisfied with what he saw, slammed the door and got into the driver's seat and started up the engine.

The van slowly nudged out into the street and accelerated away to its unknown destination. Inside, the dogs were frightened and quiet, awaiting whatever fate was in store for them. Jack, still reeling from seeing his dead mother, was feeling unwell. The van lurched as it accelerated then braked and turned around corners and soon he was feeling very ill indeed. His mouth started to water and waves of nausea overcame him until he vomited on the floor of the cage. The lurching of the van continued and he found it difficult to keep his feet in the cage and slid around in the slimy pool of vomit. As his fear increased, he let go of his bladder and bowels so that by the time the van finally drew to a standstill and the engine was turned off he was coated in urine, vomit and faeces and shaking violently.

Chapter Twenty Two

A very sorry state met the eyes of the pet inspectors when they opened up the back of the van. The woman peered into Jack's cage and recoiled at the stench of the vomit and faeces. "I think we'd better get this one sorted out quickly," she said, holding her head away from the smell and picking up his cage. She carried it into a long, low building and down a corridor until they reached a door at the end. She opened the door to reveal a tiled room with a large sink in one corner and bottles and piles of towels sitting on a table in another corner. Inside the room were two humans, each wearing plastic aprons over their clothes and rubber gloves on their hands. "Think this one needs a bath!" she said, putting the cage on the table then leaving the room.

The two humans looked carefully at the cage, nodded at each other and one of them undid the catch on the front and reached inside to pull out the shaking, shivering small dog inside.

Jack was in a sorry state indeed. He was shivering with fear and his coat, already torn and pulled out by the cats and with clumps scratched out by his attempts to dislodge fleas, was now smeared with his own vomit and faeces. With ears and tail down, he shrank back when a human reached into the cage to grab him and flinched under her touch.

"What have we got here?" the human asked of nobody in particular but looking at Jack. "Oh dear, a smelly little doggy," she said kindly. She held him up in her hands and checked his label. "I see we've got a little boy doggy under this hair, we'd better get you cleaned up then." She carried him over to the corner of the room and placed him in the sink then, together with her companion, started to use a shower contraption to run warm water over Jack's shivering body. They worked quickly and efficiently, adding shampoo to his body and massaging it gently yet thoroughly into his fur. She noted his poor condition and the fleas that scurried about in his fur, but for now the priority was to clean him up so he would be more comfortable and could be properly assessed.

His bath completed, the water was turned off and Jack was wrapped in a towel and his fur rubbed to remove the worst of the water whilst one of the humans used a hose attachment to swill down and clean his cage. Once this was clean and dry, a fresh towel was placed inside and a quivering Jack was returned to it. Bang on time, the previous human returned and, thanking her colleagues, picked up Jack's cage, saying something about "taking him to see the vet next".

Jack crouched in his cage, still shivering from his bath and with fear of the unknown. He was carried back along the corridor and then into a room in which stood a large man behind a table which was covered with thick black rubber. *This must be the vet,* thought Jack and shook a bit harder still.

The vet opened the cage door and once again an unwilling Jack was hauled out then placed on the table. The large man ran his hands over Jack's body and prodded and poked him all over. While the woman held the tiny dog, the vet parted Jack's hair and looked at his flea ridden skin, put a metal object on his chest and listened to his heart then looked into his eyes and mouth and inspected his claws. He ran a scanner across Jack's body several times then shook his head. "No chip," he said, then placed Jack on a table top weighing machine. "Three kilograms, a bit underweight" he muttered.

Apparently satisfied he tapped for several minutes into a laptop computer, then pulled out several syringes. Jack sank lower on the table and looked at the man with scared eyes. The vet paid little attention and grabbed the scruff of Jack's neck and quickly injected the contents of the syringes in, followed by half a tablet which he placed in Jack's open mouth and waited until he gulped it down. Then he placed a few drops of a liquid onto the fur at the back of Jack's neck and pushed him back into his cage before the small dog had time to argue.

"So that's sorted. The dog seems like a nice type and basically healthy but I've given him a wormer, his first inoculations and a flea treatment, together with an injection to stop him scratching. He'll need to be castrated which we can do later this week, I can microchip him and trim his claws at the same time. He can go to kennels and be fed now." The vet turned back to his laptop and finished tapping in notes.

The woman nodded and picked up the cage once more and turned to the door. Again, Jack was carried down the long corridor and then out into the fresh air. Outside they crossed a small courtyard and Jack could hear barking dogs as they approached another low building. *This must be the kennels* he thought as the woman opened a door and they entered into a passageway that ran along the back of small room-like pens, each with tiled floors and an outside, caged run attached.

Some of the pens were empty but others had dogs in them, a large golden retriever in one and a bulldog in the next. They came to the next pen and two small dogs jumped up at the pen window, yapping excitedly.

Jack immediately recognised George with his long ginger fur and Norris with his enormous sticky up ears. "Ah here we are," the woman said. "And here are your friends too. You're going to be sharing so I hope you'll all behave."

She opened the door to the pen and walked inside. Setting Jack's cage down she noted how the dogs approached it in a friendly manner and so she opened the cage door and Jack came bounding out, wagging his tail and happy to see friendly faces. "I see you're happy to be here, I'll leave you all to settle and bring some food in a little while."

Jack was so excited to see his friends he barely noticed the woman leave the pen with his empty cage and close the door behind herself. He wagged his small tail enthusiastically and sniffed his friends. They were equally pleased to see him and sniffed and snuffled around him with great joy.

Norris was first to speak, "Jack, great to see you! And you don't smell as bad now!"

Jack was surprised but remembered the journey in the van and retching and heaving so badly. Norris had been in a cage next to him there and had whispered words of encouragement. He wagged his tail again and play-nipped Norris on the shoulder. "Cheeky! I don't suppose I do, but I can't say the same for you. Phewee you two still stink!"

It was true, the other dogs had been checked over briefly after their journeys then placed straight in the kennels, the time for their baths and vet checks had yet to come.

Oblivious to this fate as yet, Norris teased his cousin, "Special treatment for you then Jack, did they wash you?"

Jack shuddered as he remembered the scary room with the sink and the hands holding him and pouring water over his body. But he also remembered the care taken to massage his sore body and lift him into a warm towel. *Perhaps it wasn't so bad after all* he thought. "Yes they did," he nodded, "but it was OK." Then he added grimly, "Better than the vet."

Norris ignored the last comment and tugged playfully at Jack's ear. "C'mon then! Let me show you the new place." He scampered off and Jack laughed and followed him with George tagging along at the back.

First stop was the water bowl where Jack gratefully drank the clean, cool water. *Ooh that was good!* Then Norris showed him the bed, a plastic dog bed with clean bedding in it. They would be snug and warm in there. Then he led the way out through a hatch into the outside run. This run had wire cage sides and Jack could see and hear the dog neighbours in their runs excitedly barking still. On one side a lumbering bulldog sniffed closely at the bars, slobber drooling down his face. Jack was spooked by the big dog and snarled at him. The bulldog ignored him and wandered back inside, Jack calmed down feeling a bit foolish. On the other side the run was empty and opposite Jack could see runs filled with dogs of different shapes and sizes, none of which he recognised.

"Where are the others?" Jack asked.

Norris shook his head, "I dunno. We haven't seen or heard anyone we know since we were dropped off, we don't even know if the other cages were unloaded here."

The dogs continued their exploration of the run, sniffing in all the corners and, where necessary, cocking their legs, just to show it belonged to them. After a final inspection they heard the door to the pen being opened and three small bowls of dog food were placed on the floor, one for each of them. "Dinner boys!" was shouted as they rushed towards the food and started to gobble it up hungrily.

It was a mix of dry dog food crunchies and meat. Jack ate the meat hurriedly, then filled his mouth with as many crunchies as he could carry and took them away to a quiet corner where he spat them out and ate them one by one. Norris and George ignored him and carried on eating at the bowls, Jack had always been funny with his food that way.

After their meal was finished, the three dogs went and lay down in the dog bed, snuggled and warm together. The noises in the kennels slowly quietened as other dogs ate their meals and settled down. The sky grew dark and the small dogs fell into a deep and well deserved sleep, exhausted after the events of the previous night and their long day.

Jack dreamed again. He was looking for his mother and couldn't find her. He ran and ran and called out for her, then he was falling. His paws twitched and he made small woofs. Norris, annoyed at being roused, nudged him and he briefly awoke, unsure where he was. *Dreaming again!* He remembered where he was and felt Norris nuzzling him which calmed him down. Jack turned around and snuggled back into the bed, his legs tucked under him and his nose pressed against George's warm back and fell back asleep. This time there were no dreams.

Chapter Twenty Three

Maisie woke up with a start, opened her eyes and then remembered where she was. The events of the previous day came flooding back to her as she lay, half awake and half dreaming. The cage containing herself and Elsie had been taken swiftly out of the house and she hadn't had time to say goodbye properly to her friends. Quivering with fear, she had clung to Elsie's side as the cage was lifted into the van, the doors slammed and the journey started.

After a period of lurching and swaying they had arrived at their destination and the cages had been lifted out once more. Elsie and Maisie had been carried across a small courtyard and past several low buildings until they entered a corridor with pens on each side. Their cage was placed in one of these and the door opened. Elsie, practical as usual, had suggested they may as well check the place out and so Maisie had timidly followed her out of the cage and into the kennel.

The kennel was clean and tidy with a bed filled with fresh bedding in the centre and a full water bowl placed in the corner. Both small dogs had sniffed suspiciously then cautiously lapped at the water, thirsty after their journey. It seemed they were the first to arrive in this row of kennels, but soon the other pens filled up with anxious dogs. Maisie spied Ruby a few pens away, morosely walking around her pen and sniffing in all the corners. Next door, Sue arrived, still calling anxiously for Stu but pleased to see faces she recognised. In the pen on Maisie's other side Betsy appeared, yapping excitedly as she too recognised old companions.

They had joined in the barking, then eaten hungrily when food arrived, two separate bowls, one for each of them and both filled with a little meat and some crunchies. Once replete and after a final turn around the outside pen they had sunk into the clean, soft bedding and fallen into a long, dreamless sleep, only waking when the light of dawn glimmered through the glass of the pen door.

As Maisie shifted, Elsie too woke up and stretched out her short legs and long back. "Morning Maisie, I wonder what's in store for us today."

Maisie shuddered. "I don't know, but I'm not sure I'm going to like it."

"Nonsense. Here we are, all comfortable and well fed, what could possibly be wrong with that?" Elsie was positive. "Now I wonder if they bring breakfast too?"

Maisie warmed to that idea. "Yes the food last night was rather good, wasn't it?" She added with a wry smile, "Let's see if the others are up yet." Her smile broadened further as she had an idea, "We shall call for breakfast!"

They both got up out of the warm bed and wandered out into the run where they walked around, sniffing in the corners and relieving themselves. Sue was already out in her run, anxiously staring around, and Betsy was a little slower in getting up but dashed outside when she saw Elsie and Maisie appear.

Maisie explained to her neighbours her idea of how they were going to call for breakfast and then, on her signal, all four dogs started to bark. Other dogs in the kennel heard them bark and came out to bark themselves. A cacophony of barking spread throughout the kennels and rippled around a few times until it finally died out. "There," said Maisie, smiling triumphantly, " they'll bring us some breakfast now!"

Indeed, the barking did seem to prompt some human activity. Humans appeared and opened pen doors and placed new food dishes out for the dogs. Maisie, well pleased with her work, guzzled up her breakfast in front of an amused Elsie. She was beginning to like this place after all.

Maisie had just settled back in her bed, smugly pleased with herself, when the pen door was opened, a human appeared and, without warning, scooped her up and popped her into a carrying basket. "Help me! Elsie, do something!" she cried as the basket swung in the air. Elsie dashed forward but she was too late. With a practised ease borne of handling many frightened dogs in a calm and assertive manner, the human swept the basket containing the tiny dog up and out of the pen and closed the kennel door smartly behind them. Elsie could only stare at the closed door and call sadly after her friend.

Meanwhile Maisie was dangling in mid air in the basket. She cowered low inside as the basket swung gently from side to side as the human carried it out of the kennels, into another building, along a corridor and into a side room. There, yet another human stood behind a large and ominous looking table and looked expectantly as the door to the room opened. A smaller table was placed at the back of the room, upon which sat a laptop computer and there was a cupboard on the wall above it, with bottles and scary looking implements showing dimly through the smoked glass doors. The basket was lifted onto the table, the door flap opened and then a hand reached inside to lift the tiny quivering dog out. "Oooo noooo" squealed Maisie, blinking wildly as she was lifted out into the bright lights of the vet's examining room.

The vet was gentle but thorough. Maisie was carefully examined from nose to tail, with firm hands turning her around, parting her fur, opening her mouth and feeling her tummy, then lights were shone into her eyes and ears. A cold metal button with wires attached to the vet's ears made her jump when it was pressed against her chest to listen to her heart. Finally the vet made a prognosis. "Fine little dog this! Needs a little clean up - worming, flea treatment and nail trim, and could you schedule her for neuter and microchipping please?" He turned and tapped some details into the laptop before rummaging in the cupboard and turning back to Maisie with a scary looking syringe in his hand. "I'll just get her vaccinations started now," he said and smoothly grabbed Maisie by the scruff of the neck, popping the syringe into her fur before she could even think to protest. "There! You can go for your bath now." He nodded and the human who was holding Maisie swept her up back into the carrying basket and, before she could utter further protest, she was off on her travels once more.

Slightly disoriented, Maisie crouched low as she was carried out into the corridor and then into another room with tiles and a large sink. Here, there was another human and together they lifted Maisie out of the basket and into the sink. Gently, they washed the small, shaking dog, trimmed her claws with nail clippers, persuaded her to swallow a small worming tablet and squirted anti flea treatment on the back of her neck. All done, she was wrapped in a large, warm towel and settled back into her basket, ready to go again. "There, all pretty now," said the human, admiring their handiwork, "I'll take you back to your kennel now," and swung the basket up once more and carried it along the corridor to the kennel.

Maisie was set down in the kennel and the basket opened. She jumped out with relief and quickly hurried away from the human. The kennel had been cleaned, the tiles smelt of fresh disinfectant and new bedding had been placed in the bed. She lapped eagerly at the fresh bowl of water that had been placed in one corner and slowly realised that Elsie was not there.

Wildly, she looked around the pen. "Elsie! Elsie, where are you?" she called. She ran around the walls and caged sides of the kennel, calling desperately for her friend.

Just as she completed a second lap, the door opened and a human entered the pen again. A carrier was placed on the floor and a small brown nose pushed its way out. It was Elsie, back from the vet and her bath and looking mightily pleased with herself. "What's all this noise? What's all the fuss about, Maisie?"

Elsie waddled out of the carrier, making sure that her long back and all of her paws were out, before turning and wagging her tail at the human. "Thank You human!" she barked as the human patted her head and picked up the carrier before turning to go. "You see, Maisie, nothing to worry about." She stretched out one paw and examined it carefully. "The humans gave me a bath and massaged my itchy back. Why, they even trimmed my nails!"

Maisie heaved a sigh of relief. "Oh Elsie, I thought you'd gone. Vanished. Disappeared... like... like Jack's mum." She shuddered as she remembered the limp and lifeless body being carried out of the house.

Elsie, knowing that Maisie had had a fright and not wanting to dwell on too many horrors of times past, decided that her friend needed a distraction. "No, just a little bath. In fact it's just like one of those hotel things the human used to talk about. Nice room, good food and it seems..." She looked around at the newly tidied kennel and sniffed up the smell of disinfectant. "It Seems like we have maid service too!" She walked over to the bed and pulled an item from under a blanket. "See Maisie, they've even left us toys!" She lay down and holding a small red rubber bone between her front paws, started to chew.

"What? Wait for me Elsie! I didn't know about toys." Maisie tried to grab the bone from Elsie, but the Dachshund was too quick for her and twisted away. "Humph!" said Maisie. "There must be some more, I'll have a look." Sure enough, she had a dig in the bed and came out triumphant. "Look Elsie, look!" she squealed between clenched teeth as she held a small ball in her jaws. She dropped it on the floor and it rolled away. Maisie gave another squeal of delight and ran after it.

The two small dogs spent the rest of the morning playing with their toys. Elsie was content to chew the small rubber bone whilst lying quietly in her bed, but for Maisie the party had only just started.

Chapter Twenty Four

Maisie had discovered a great game. She dropped the ball at one end of the pen and watched it roll, faster and faster down the sloped floor until it stopped with a clang and a bounce at the bars at the other end of the pen. Over and over she fetched it back, dropped it and watched it roll. Betsy next door was fascinated by this and ran alongside the bars, snapping at the ball, but never managing to catch it.

The two small dogs were thoroughly enjoying their game, wrapped up entirely in the excitement of the chase, and so didn't notice they were being watched until a human voice interrupted their game.

"Dad, Dad, look at that one! Dad, come over here quickly!" A small human stood on the other side of the bars, looking intently at Maisie who stopped playing with the ball to stare shyly back.

A larger human ambled over to stand behind them. "What's that, Tom? What've you seen?"

Tom pointed at Maisie. "Look at that little dog, Dad. She's so clever, she's been making a game for the other dog!"

Tom's dad looked down at his son, saw the animation in his face and a slow smile spread over his own. He said nothing but peered into the pen in front of him. He could see two dogs inside, one was lying in a dog bed, chewing a toy but the other one, at which Tom was pointing, was stood bang in the middle of the pen and staring back at them. He put his hand on Tom's shoulder. "I'll get your mum."

"No need, I'm already here." Another voice chimed in and another human appeared outside the pen. She too looked at Tom and the same slow smile lit her face. "Now Tom, show me what you're looking at."

Tom, delighted he had his parents' attention, stooped down and put his face near to the bars of the pen. "Here little doggie," he called.

Maisie, frightened of the humans, but somehow mesmerised by the voice of the small one, slowly walked forwards. Tom pushed his fingers through the bars and Maisie cautiously sniffed them. "Careful," Tom's dad called, "we don't know if she'll nip."

Maisie, however, had other ideas. This small human connected with her, she could see the sadness in his eyes, hidden behind the searching look as he scanned her face. *He too has lost a loved one.* She wanted to make him happy again, wanted to help him forget his grief and she slowly opened her small mouth to reveal a set of tiny, razor sharp teeth.

"Tom, please be careful, she may bite!" Tom's mum was anxious. She needn't have worried though for Maisie simply started to lick the fingers of this sad but kind boy and he wiggled them slowly in response.

Tom had made up his mind. "This one, Dad, I want this one." Then he remembered his manners and stuttered out, "...that is... er... please can I have this one?"

Dad hesitated. "I don't know if we can, the staff told us not to look in these kennels, the dogs haven't yet been properly assessed. Why don't we go and look at some other dogs?"

Tom looked mutinous for a moment, but he didn't want to disobey his father, so after a brief internal struggle he shrugged his shoulders and turned back to Maisie. Maisie was now sitting down in front of him and offering him her ball. "I'll be back for you, don't worry," he whispered.

Tom stood up and the family then turned and walked back along the row of kennels and went out of sight. A fresh wave of dogs barking could be heard from the kennels around the corner.

"Maisie, are you alright?" Elsie had stopped chewing her toy and had waddled over to her friend. "You look, er, thoughtful?"

Maisie was sitting very still and was looking in the direction of where the boy had gone. She had dropped her ball at her feet and it had rolled into the corner of the pen, it now held no interest for her. "He knew," she said simply, "he knew how I felt."

Meanwhile Tom followed his parents around the corner of the kennels and tried to look interested as they looked into the individual kennels at a mixture of dogs. There were large dogs, small dogs, even medium dogs. Friendly dogs with wagging tails, reserved, anxious dogs gazing at him shyly as they passed but none of the dogs connected with him in the same way that the tiny, cream chihuahua had. His face fell and the sad expression returned once more.

Dad, seeing the sad look return, bent down and put his arm around Tom's shoulder. "What's up Tom? Don't you like the look of any of these dogs?"

Tom was unsure what to say. He couldn't get the image of Maisie out of his mind, but he didn't want to disappoint his parents. He knew they had brought him there to choose a dog for the whole family. He knew also they were trying to cheer him up and that he should make an effort. He turned to the nearest pen where a medium, tan coloured dog was wagging its tail at him. He thought the dog looked friendly, but he didn't want to take it home with him. He could imagine feeding it and going for walks with it, but not sitting stroking it and telling it his innermost thoughts. He couldn't imagine this dog understanding.

He turned away.

Dad saw the valiant effort his son made, saw the sadness returning and he remembered how animated he had been when he had met the tiny Chihuahua. "Okay, I guess we'd better go and find out about the other little dog then. Let's go and find someone to ask."

Tom rewarded him with a wide smile. "Thanks Dad."

"No promises, mind. We don't know why we weren't meant to look at her. She may already be taken." Then, seeing Tom's face fall again, he quickly added, "But maybe not. Let's find out."

Fortuitously, at that moment, a member of staff walked along the row of kennels towards them. "Excuse me," Dad stepped forward to intercept. "My son has set his heart on a tiny cream dog from around the corner. I know we weren't meant to view those dogs, but is there any chance she may be available?"

Rachel had had a very busy morning. They had received a large contingent of new dogs the previous day and were still sorting them out, organising vet visits, assessments and just making sure the dogs were settled. She knew those new dogs were not yet ready for viewing, let alone being allocated to new homes. She felt inclined to brush the query off, there were plenty of other dogs needing a home.

However, she too had noticed the timid little chihuahua and there was something about the earnest question and the look of hope in the little boy's face that made her pause as the family waited for her reply. She decided on a non-committal answer. "I really shouldn't as the dogs aren't ready yet, but I could ask for you. You could check back with us in a few days." She prepared to walk on, she had lots to do.

Tom held his breath and Mum and Dad looked more optimistic. Rachel looked at the family, the three of them watching her, hopeful and waiting. She sighed and capitulated, "Tell you what, follow me now to the office and I'll take some details."

She waved for them to follow her as she walked back along the row of kennels, across a small courtyard and opened a door on the side of a low building. They stepped inside a small room with a tiled floor and a desk and two chairs in one corner.

Rachel sat down on one of the chairs and motioned to Tom's dad to be seated on the other chair. She switched on the computer and as it started to whir into life she looked across the desk. "Now Mr. er....?"

"Jackson, it's Alan Jackson. This is my wife, Sonia and my son, Tom." Dad nodded to his family.

The computer finished whirring and Rachel nodded and clicked the mouse. "Right Mr. Jackson," she said. Then, smiling at the others, she added, "And Mrs Jackson and Tom, of course. I'll need to take some details, let's start with your address."

Steadily Rachel asked questions and Dad answered them, with the occasional nod of agreement from his wife and interjection from Tom when he didn't think the urgency of securing the small Chihuahua was being addressed. "Dad, ask her if we can have the small dog we saw. I only want that one."

Rachel laughed at his impatience and turned to speak to him. "All in good time, Tom, we need to get the boring bits sorted out first and to make sure that your family and Maisie will suit each other."

Maisie! Tom mouthed the name silently. *So that's the small dog's name.* He thought for a moment then his eyes lit up. *It suits her. Maisie, Maisie, Maisie. Oh please let her come home with us!*

Rachel turned back to the computer and tapped in a few more details. "Now Tom," she said, turning to look at him, "Maisie has only just come in to us and we will need a few days to settle her and make proper assessments. You're going to have to be very patient whilst we do all this, do you think you can do that?"

Tom, desperate to do anything to make sure of getting his beloved Maisie, gulped and nodded.

"Good!" Rachel turned back to Tom's parents. "Right then, Mr and Mrs Jackson, we'll hurry along those assessments and if they go alright, we'll contact you to come back in and formally meet Maisie and get the adoption process going." She stood up and walked to open the office door. "I'll be in touch."

The family stood up, thanked her and walked out of the office. Rachel watched them go. *Lots of things to get organised,* she thought and strode purposefully over to the kennel block.

Chapter Twenty Five

Jack woke up, opened his eyes and stretched. *Ouch!* He'd forgotten about his wounds and his body ached when he moved. His eyes slowly focussed and he remembered where he was. His nose was pressed against Norris's fur and something was digging into his back. *George! It must be George's paw.* As he moved he woke his companions, and they too uncurled and stretched out.

Norris was first to speak. "I wonder what will happen today? Perhaps we'll get more of that lovely food." He paused, remembering. "Oh yes, I hope there's more food."

Jack laughed, "You and food!" As he said it, a distant barking started and like a wave it drew closer, until they could hear the dogs in the pens next to them join in.

"Food, food, food," they barked, "bring us food!"

"Might as well join in," muttered George, shaking out his whiskers, and the three small dogs rushed outside into the run and started to bark for food too.

Their efforts were soon rewarded with the sound of humans moving about, opening kennel doors and placing bowls on the tiled floors. They could hear them getting nearer, until, at last the door to their kennel opened and three bowls of food were placed next to the bed.

"Yippee!" yelled Norris and rushed over to the nearest bowl and started to guzzle. Jack and George looked at each other, laughed then hurried over to start eating at a more leisurely pace. As before, Jack removed some of the dry crunchies and buried them in the bed. *Just in case.*

Once breakfast was eaten, the small dogs went back out into the run to sniff around and relieve themselves. There wasn't much to see out there, their neighbours still seemed to be eating, so they went back to the bed for a post breakfast snooze.

Some time later in mid morning, the door to the pen opened and a human appeared with two dog carriers in her hands. She placed them on the floor, opened them up and approached the small dogs. She quickly picked up Jack and put him into one and deftly captured Norris and George and popped them into the other. "Now little doggies, time to get you all sorted out."

She carried them out of the kennel and, dogs shaking in the swinging carriers, out into another building and along a corridor. She stopped at the open doorway to one room and placed the carrier with Jack Chi in it on the floor. "Here's your first one, Rachel, I'm taking the other two for vet and clean up," she announced and walked off down the corridor, a single carrier now swinging from her arm.

Inside the room, Rachel softly closed the door and then knelt down on the floor and carefully opened the carrier. Jack sat inside, quivering. "There now little doggy, nothing to worry about," soothed Rachel and reached a hand inside. Jack nervously licked it and allowed the human to pick him up and pull him onto her lap.

Rachel looked at the shaking dog on her knee. Ears flattened and tail down, the whites of his eyes showing, she noted a frightened little dog. Although bathed, fed and rested, he was missing clumps of hair all over and several nasty scratches were slowly healing. "Dear, dear, little one, what a mess. Now, nothing to be scared about, I'm just going to check some things out and see what sort of little doggy we've got and what type of home we need to find for you."

Jack couldn't understand a word she said, of course, but she was calm and soothing and he rather liked her. He settled some more onto her knee and gave her face a lick. Rachel laughed. "Well I can see you're friendly and like to lick!"

She put Jack on the floor and reached up to a table, bringing a small tray of interesting items down. She put the tray on the floor beside her and picked up a small object. It was a ball. She offered it to Jack who sniffed it suspiciously, then took it from her outstretched hand and dropped it on the floor and returned to trying to get back on her knee.

Rachel laughed and shooed him off. "Let's try that a different way then," she said and picked the ball up, gave it a little shake and rolled it across the floor. Jack begrudgingly followed it, but once it came to a stop, so did he and he returned to Rachel and gave her hand a lick.

"So you don't like balls then, Jack?" Jack looked intently at her, it was the first time he'd heard another human say his name and he rather liked it. He looked adoringly at her face and tried to climb onto her knee. He liked sitting on knees and laps, he felt safe there. Rachel, however, had other ideas. She pushed him away and picked up another object from the tray. Jack stared. This was a small furry item, a bit like the catnip mice he and Norris had played with, only a bit bigger and not so smelly. He sniffed the toy and opened his mouth to take it from Rachel. Rachel let him take it and he pulled away and sat down with this toy. It was soft and made of a furry material and crackled when he bit it. Bite, crackle, bite, crackle, bite, bite, bite. *Oh yes!* Jack threw the toy up and pounced on it when it landed. Bite, crackle, bite. He wagged his small tail, bite, crackle, pounce, bite.

Rachel watched him silently and let him play with the toy for a while. She reached up for a file of papers and a pen and wrote down some words. Tiring of his game after a little while, Jack approached Rachel and placed the toy on her knee. "Oh, you do want to play then," Rachel picked up the soggy toy and threw it across the floor. Slipping and sliding on the tiles, Jack chased after it and pounced once more. Rachel noticed how he watched the toy, how his little legs worked to keep him upright on the slippery floor, how his tail wagged all the time and then she made some more notes.

They played for a little more time until both of them grew a bit tired. Rachel reached in her trouser pocket and brought out a small meaty smelling item. "Now let's see what training you know."

Jack dropped the toy, sniffed the offered treat and took it from Rachel. He carried it across the room and placed it on the floor. Rachel picked the toy up and put it back in the tray. Cautiously, Jack started to eat the treat, *mmmm tasty.*

"Jack come!" Rachel called. Jack pricked his ears at the sound of her voice, but didn't move. "Jack, come here!" Rachel repeated the command and clapped her hands. Jack, attracted by the sound, went towards her. *Perhaps she's got more treats.* Rachel reached into her pocket once more and gave him another treat. *I could get to like you,* mused Jack, chewing then swallowing the treat quickly and gazing lovingly at his new friend.

Next, Rachel put out her hand and commanded, "Sit!" Jack continued to stand, a look of adoration in his eyes, but he didn't move. "Sit, Jack!" He stayed still. Rachel reached for another treat, she had his whole attention now, he wagged his tail. "Sit!" she pressed one hand on his bottom and held the treat high in the other. Jack lifted his nose to sniff the treat and, *Oooh dear!* He found himself sliding forward and sitting on his bottom. "Good boy!" announced Rachel and gave him the treat to eat. She reached for her pen once more and wrote in her pad. "Not trained but trainable," she muttered quietly as she wrote. Jack licked her hand and wagged his little tail hopefully.

Rachel stood up and went over to the far wall to a series of hooks. Jack followed her and watched as she selected a lead and a harness. She bent down and tried to put the harness on the small dog. Jack was very scared and wriggled hard, not putting his head or paws through the harness at the right moments. He'd met his match though and, after a brief struggle and a bit of light wrestling, Rachel was successful and Jack was harnessed and attached to a lead. Rachel, straightening up and still puffing slightly from the struggle, announced, "Now we're going to see what else you know." Jack simply licked her leg and cautiously wagged his tail.

Rachel pulled on the lead and Jack came towards her. She walked across the floor and opened the door, Jack followed. They walked along the corridor, Jack carefully putting one paw in front of the other, keeping one eye on Rachel. As they reached the end of the corridor Rachel opened a door and stepped out into a yard, Jack followed, a tiny little ball of fur trotting along to keep up with the human's long strides. They crossed the yard and entered an enclosed area with caged sides and green matting on the floor.

Rachel closed the cage door behind her and greeted another human who was sitting across on the other side of the green stuff. The other human had a large dog beside her who she was playing with. Jack gasped as he immediately recognised the dog, *Titan!* The staffie looked up at the newcomers and curled his lip. "Welcome to the play area, Jack," he snarled. Titan was feeling particularly aggrieved. In the past 24 hours his world had crumbled. He'd been uprooted from his home, separated from the place and dogs where he held power and had been inspected and prodded and poked by humans. "Do you see what you've done, you and your rat friends?" Titan glared at the small dog. "You've brought us all to this awful place. This is all your fault and you're going to pay."

Jack shrank back, but Titan lunged closer and Jack stepped back slightly. He was a small but feisty little dog and being with

Rachel had made him feel stronger. He bravely wrinkled his nose and hissed at Titan, "My fault? It's you who are to blame. You and your big friends, you just couldn't resist the chance to hurt others to help yourselves."

Rachel, with a small, snarling dog looking as if he would attack the larger dog, quickly pulled on the lead. "Jack, no! You're supposed to make friends."

Jack glanced quickly up at her and then back to Titan. The other human had pulled the bigger dog away and was walking him out of the caged area. Jack was still upset. "You've only got yourselves to blame!" he shouted after the retreating figure of Titan. Titan, however, didn't look back.

Rachel, laughing slightly at the feisty little dog, pulled on his lead until he turned to look at her. "Well, Jack, I guess you didn't pass the meeting other dogs test then! I think we'd better find you a calmer home on your own." Jack looked adoringly at her and licked her hand.

Chapter Twenty Six

Jack was returned to his kennel, where he found everything had been cleaned up and tidied. Much to his disappointment, the crunchies he'd hidden for later were gone, as were his friends. However, he did not have long to wait before the door opened and the swinging carrier was brought in and his friends returned.

George and Norris had been checked over by the vet who had jabbed them and given out worm and flea treatments. Once they'd both been given a clean bill of health they had been taken to the room with the humans who properly cleaned them up. George was indignant, his moustache bristling, but Norris thought it was all some huge game. "Jack, we've seen the vet and had a bath! What fun!"

George inspected the bed and decided to lie down, he'd had a long morning and it had quite worn him out, but Norris and Jack were pleased to see each other and playfully pulled at each other's ears and wagging tails with their teeth. Finally, they settled down and had a drink of water, then Jack told his friends of his morning, his time with the human, Rachel, and the meeting with Titan.

Over the next week all the dogs settled into a routine of sorts. They were roused in the morning by Maisie who always started barking for food and they all joined in, lest it didn't arrive. Then there was usually some sort of outing whilst their kennels were cleaned, followed by restful afternoons, regular tea and bedtime.

The activities ranged from various trips to have behaviour and training assessed and general health trips to check wounds were healing and flea treatments were working. There were also the ominous neutering trips to the vet where the shaking dogs were put into a deep sleep and operations to remove any further chance of unwanted puppies were carried out. During these operations the vet also checked teeth, claws and inserted a microchip in each dog's neck. The dogs returned to their cleaned up kennels groggy and sore and with strange cones around their necks. With clean beds for pleasant afternoon naps and plenty of good food for tea they soon bounced back.

After the first week, the visitors started to be allowed to inspect the new dogs. The humans came and looked through the bars, talked between themselves and pointed at various dogs. The dogs, depending on their individual temperaments, barked and wagged their tails, ran away and played shy or simply ignored the visitors and carried on snoozing.

At the end of each afternoon, tea was served and the dogs ate hungrily then fell into long sleeps in their beds at night.

Rachel, meanwhile, had more pressing things on her mind. After her meeting with Tom's family she had pressed forward with getting Maisie assessed and treated by the vet. Maisie had passed all tests with flying colours and had recovered well from her neutering. Rachel was ready to ring her potential new owners and start the formal adoption process. She sat in the office and picked up the phone, dialled the number and waited for it to be picked up. "Hello, is that Mr Jackson?"

Tom's dad answered the phone, he was delighted to hear from her. Yes they were still very interested in adopting Maisie, indeed Tom hadn't stopped talking about her since the day they'd visited and, of course, they wanted to go ahead. Rachel was pleased to hear this and agreed to organise a couple of things. Firstly, the family would come in and meet Maisie properly, then they would complete the paperwork and pay a deposit. Next, Rachel would arrange for a home inspection and, all being well, the adoption would go right ahead very soon.

The very next afternoon Tom's family turned up at the kennels, excited about meeting Maisie properly. Rachel welcomed them and showed them into the room where she'd previously sat with them to take details and asked them to wait. She disappeared for a little while and returned with a tiny dog on a lead. Tom, who'd been trying to contain his excitement, jumped up at the sight of Maisie once more, causing her to cringe away and hide behind Rachel's legs.

Rachel smiled. "Careful Tom, she's a bit shy. Just stay still for a moment."

Tom did as he was told and the whole family held their breaths as the tiny Chihuahua peeked out from behind Rachel's legs and looked at Tom.

Maisie recognised the small human who had played with her on that first day. *He's back!* She tried to be brave but it was difficult with all these humans in the room and she was still feeling a bit sore after her trip to the vet during the previous week. She very shyly walked around Rachel's leg and went across to the small boy. Tom looked at her and then back to Rachel who nodded and signalled he could bend down to greet the dog. Tom knelt down and extended his hand towards the timid little dog who sniffed him slowly and then decided he was a friend.

Maisie wagged her tail and looked up at his face, Tom beamed. "Good girl, Maisie!" Maisie wagged her tail faster and put a paw on his knee. Tom stroked her neck and then gave her back a little scratch in just the right place. Maisie, forgetting her soreness and wriggling with excitement, threw all caution to the wind and climbed on his knee in ecstasy. A good few minutes were then spent with Tom stroking and scratching the little dog and Maisie wriggling in return and frantically wagging her tail.

Rachel was relieved, she'd become fond of the shy but valiant Chihuahua and hoped she'd get a good home. This, however, went further than she'd hoped for and looked like it was going to be perfect. After the scratching and wriggling frenzy abated, Maisie sat on Tom's knee and looked around her. Dad quietly walked forward and bent down so he could reach Maisie. Slowly, he extended his hand until Maisie sniffed it, then he reached for the same spot on her back that Tom had scratched and gave it a little stroke. Maisie closed her eyes in triumph, *This!* Dad stepped back to let his wife gently walk forward and stoop to repeat the stroke. Maisie was even more impressed. *All these humans to pamper me!*

"I think she's made up her mind then Tom!" Rachel was pleased. She showed Tom how to gently put Maisie on the floor in front of him and handed him a small treat to give her. Maisie waited patiently whilst the small boy looked at the treat and then offered it to her. She took it from him carefully, making sure not to touch those precious fingers with her teeth, and chewed it up hungrily. *That's tasty for sure.*

The family spent a bit of time getting to know Maisie and listening to Rachel who gave them some pointers on how to deal with the small dog who knew nothing of the world.

Tom knew a little bit about dogs, he'd helped his grandad look after and walk his Jack Russell, Bertie until old Bertie had become too ill and died. Sadly, a few months later, Grandad had also died and Tom still felt the loss of him keenly every day. A few months later still, this had been the reasoning behind his parents' decision to adopt a new dog. They wanted to see the sad look in Tom's eyes replaced. When he'd first seen Maisie, that sadness had vanished for a while and his parents knew she would be a perfect companion for the morose little boy.

Maisie had won all of their hearts and she shyly succumbed to the family's fussing and treat feeding of her whilst Rachel outlined the next steps. They could fill in the adoption form fully now and pay a deposit then she would arrange a home check and hopefully they would be able to take Maisie home in the next few days. Tom beamed and looked hopefully at his dad. "Can we, Dad? Can we pleeease?"

Everyone's eyes were on Dad, even Maisie stopped wriggling for a moment and turned her dark brown eyes on him. Dad paused for just a moment, then he said, "Of course we can!" and everyone breathed again.

Rachel jumped into action, explaining that she would return Maisie to her kennel first and then they would sort out the rest of the process. She tempted Maisie begrudgingly off Tom's knee and led her out of the room and back to the kennels before returning to sort out the application.

Tom's mum and dad completed the adoption paperwork and Dad reached for his bank card to pay the deposit. Rachel quickly checked the calendar and suggested the home check could be done on the next day if they were available. A bit of juggling later and yes that was suitable. Tom could hardly contain his excitement. *Maisie was coming home!*

Rachel hummed happily to herself after Tom's family left, she had a really good feeling about this one. There was lots more work to do, of course, as she still had homes to find for so many dogs.

She walked back over to the kennels and was met by a couple of people who wanted to ask her a question. The first one, an older lady, stopped her and asked, "We've just been looking at the dogs, can you tell me which ones are available?"

Rachel looked at the lady and her companion, a younger man, and correctly judged them to be mother and son. "Certainly. Which dogs are you interested in?"

The lady replied, "We're looking for a small dog and have just seen those in that kennel." She motioned with her hand towards the kennel with Jack, George and Norris in. All three dogs were jumping up at the bars and wagging their tails excitedly.

"Well, they're all available, which one did you have in mind?"

"I like the white one best, then the long haired ginger one and then the smooth haired one, in that order, but which do you think would be suitable for us?" the lady asked. "I'm looking for a small dog as I've got the time and would like the company as I've just retired." She gestured towards the young man beside her. "My son, Joe, suggested the white one would be best."

Rachel considered for a minute, she knew Jack was probably the most nervous as he had reacted to dogs and people when she'd assessed him. However, this seemed like a good adult home with someone who had time to spend on the small dog. "I think the white one may suit, perhaps we can go into the office to get a few details and perhaps meet him properly? If you two go over there, I'll bring the dog in a minute." She gestured back across the yard towards the office door.

"Certainly, we'll pop over there now then," the lady said and she and Joe started to walk towards the office whilst Rachel went into the kennels to fetch Jack.

Jack had been excited to see the visitors. Along with George and Norris, he had dashed up to the kennel bars, barking and wagging his small tail. The two humans had seemed delighted to meet them and had talked between themselves somewhat. Jack had caught a few words, "cute", "sort of dog we're looking for" and "surely he's already taken" as the humans looked him over. He stretched his long tongue out through the bars, but the humans sensibly kept their distance so didn't get licked.

Now they had disappeared again but his friend Rachel was here, in his kennel, trying to attach a lead to his squirming body. "Come on, Jack, let me put this lead on you, I've got to show you off to the visitors," she gasped as Jack dodged and wriggled and then licked her face. "You and your tongue! Yes, I've had a wash thank you."

Eventually, they emerged from the kennels and crossed the yard to the office. As they approached the doorway, Jack grew scared and pulled back. Then he stopped and wouldn't move a step further. Rachel pulled on the lead and encouraged him, but he stood firm. Sighing gently, she bent down and picked him up. "Come on Jack, there's nothing to be scared of." She opened the door and carried him into the office.

Chapter Twenty Seven

Molly Brown had just retired. It was mid summer and the weather was warm and sultry. She had big plans for this phase of her life, now that paid work was behind her. More time to do the things she liked and time to get a little companion to share her life with.

She thought back with fondness to the dogs she'd known, most recently the black cross Labrador that had shared the family fun and chased rabbits on the fields and footpaths around their home. As a child she'd been wary but smitten by the moody, scruffy terrier of indeterminate breeding that told you in no uncertain terms to leave his ears alone and, if you didn't take notice, showed you his sharp teeth in a grimace that bordered on a snarl. Then there'd been the delicate and shy sandy dog who'd cowered at the sight of men but had slowly learned to trust her new family. All of them unwanted and rescued and given a good home until their final days. *Yes*, she thought, *I want a dog to share my retirement with.* She wanted to rehome a dog once more, a dog with a few rough edges, but who, with love and firmness could blossom once more. *Like me,* she mused with a wry inward smile.

Life had given her a few knocks recently. First a difficult divorce, the impacts on her adult children still being felt and shared in the quieter moments. There followed a move to a much smaller, more manageable house and the upheaval that had meant. Then work had announced redundancies and, after a while spent railing against it, she had given in to the inevitable and decided to take retirement early, certain she was on the scrapheap for good but quietly determined to get on with life.

So she had gone on to the website and seen the pictures of the dogs. The big dogs, the small dogs, the young and the old dogs, the dogs also thrown on the scrapheap and needing new starts. *Like me indeed.* Then she had arranged to go and view.

She'd dragged her son, Joe, along to the rescue kennels on a bright and warm summer's day and together they'd wandered up and down the rows of kennels and peered into some of them. They had both been drawn to the group of small dogs, Joe remarking on how the small, white, hairy dog looked just the sort of dog his mother would like. Both had looked at the tiny dog, standing on his hind legs and with paws up on the cage front of the kennel, wagging his tail excitedly and trying to lick their fingers through the bars.

Now they were standing waiting in the relative cool of the office, ready to meet this small, white dog.

"Here he is!" Rachel walked in the office carrying a small bundle of white fur. She put him down on the tiled floor and announced, "This is Jack."

Jack was not impressed at being put down. He liked Rachel, but who were these other humans? He wanted to be picked up again and stay with Rachel where he felt safe. He looked up at her with his soft brown eyes and clawed at her leg.

"Oh no Jack," Rachel laughed. "I'm not picking you up again. You need to meet these people."

Jack was dubious and walked behind her legs, peering shyly out at the other two humans.

"Gosh, he is tiny!" said Molly, bending down and extending a hand towards him. Jack shrank back, his ears and tail drooping down in fear. "He seems afraid, perhaps because we are all so much bigger than him?" Molly knelt down on the tiles and extended her hand again. Jack stayed behind Rachel's legs but he did give the outstretched hand a quick sniff.

"Perhaps if we all sit down at his level and let him make his mind up?" suggested Rachel and so all the humans sat down on the floor. Jack liked this game a lot more, he could see more laps to sit on. He promptly got on Rachel's knee and gave her a lick.

"Hmph!" laughed Rachel. "Perhaps we can try him with some food instead?" She popped Jack off her knee and stood up to reach onto the table for some treats. The treats were rather large so she broke them up into smaller pieces and handed one each to Molly and Joe.

Jack sniffed Joe and licked his hand. He watched as Joe offered the treat, then sniffed it cautiously. Finally he took the treat off Joe but then spat it out.

"Oh dear, not food motivated then, perhaps he just needs a bit more time." Rachel wanted to give the tiny dog every chance to overcome his shyness.

And so the humans continued sitting on the floor, waiting for Jack to get used to them. Whilst they sat, Rachel talked a bit about his background and that they would need a lot of patience and to take time to let Jack get to know them and his new home - if they were to adopt him.

Jack was unimpressed with the humans. He knew Rachel, but these new humans had scared him, they had towered over him and smelled different. He had clung to Rachel until the new humans had sat on the floor, when they had started to seem less scary. He'd sniffed the nearest one, but wasn't impressed with the hard treat offered. He had tiny teeth and not a strong jaw for chewing hard treats so he had taken it suspiciously then spat it out. The humans had started to talk between themselves so he busied himself exploring the corners of the office, keeping a weather eye on any movements made by the humans.

Jack made circuits of the office floor, slowly drawing closer to the humans who talked to each other and carefully watched him. He stopped to sniff Molly's foot then moved away again. Steadily, he drew closer and closer until he found Joe's outstretched legs. Jack loved a good lap to sit on and this was irresistible. He pawed at Joe's thigh, Joe smiled and said "Hello Jack!" encouragingly. Jack made up his mind, he liked these humans after all, so he climbed onto Joe's lap and licked his hand.

"There!" said Rachel, "that settles it, he likes you."

Indeed Jack did like these humans and for the next few minutes tried out both their laps, washed their faces with his long tongue and wagged his tail incessantly.

"No, Jack," giggled Molly, fending off his licking, "I've already had a wash today, thankyou!" Jack ignored her words, gave her another lick then curled up on her lap. Molly smiled, "I can see he's going to be a lap dog!" Little did she realise how accurate that description would turn out to be.

Satisfied that Jack was settling well with these humans, Rachel watched as they petted and played with the tiny dog.

Molly patiently searched for and found just the right spot on Jack's back to scratch him whilst he wriggled with delight. Joe tried to tempt him to play with a rubber bone which Jack studiously ignored. Rachel wracked her brains. "I think he does like toys, but softer ones. Perhaps you could try some different ones if the adoption is approved."

Finally, Rachel announced that it was time to return Jack to his kennel, before she could take forward the adoption paperwork. "That's if you want to proceed?" she asked.

Molly looked at Joe, who nodded his head eagerly. "Yes please!"

The three humans stood up, Molly carefully placing Jack on the ground in front of her. "Er, would you mind if we took a picture of Jack, before he goes back to his kennel?" she enquired.

Rachel had no objections, but picked Jack up and passed him to Molly to hold. Jack wasn't so sure about this high up feeling with the new stranger and lowered his ears and tail as Joe took out his phone and took a couple of snaps of Molly with Jack in her arms.

Jack was returned to the floor and then Rachel clipped on his lead and opened the door. "Shan't be long!"

Rachel disappeared for a few minutes before returning and taking Molly's details and reservation fee. She had just said goodbye to them both and exited the office when the next person in a long line of potential adoptees cornered her to ask about viewing "one of the dogs".

She found that the next week went by in a whirl of requests for viewings. She organised for dogs to be met by potential new owners, filled out endless paperwork, took reservation fees and started to organise home visits.

The first home visit she organised was for Maisie and a colleague provided a great report on a very suitable home for this little dog. Rachel was relieved, she so wanted Tom to have Maisie and, as it was Saturday, she rang Tom's dad immediately. "Mr Jackson, I've got good news! The home check is complete and you're now approved to finalise Maisie's adoption."

She heard a kerfuffle and the sounds of whoops of delight at the other end of the phone and she gathered that Tom had overheard. "I expect you'll be wanting to pick her up soon then?"

Dad laughed. "You bet!" he said, "I think we could come down this afternoon, if that would be convenient?"

Rachel agreed and several hours later Tom and his parents were waiting breathlessly at Reception.

Tom held in his hands a tiny pink collar with a pink, heart shaped, metal tally attached. He held it up for Rachel to see. "It's got our name and address on it, so we'll never lose her!" He explained.

Rachel invited the family into the office where she motioned to them to be seated and took out a folder which she passed to Tom's dad. "I've got the final paperwork all sorted, if you could just check through it and sign where I've indicated, then I'll take your final payment." She handed him a pen and pointed to the paper. Dad read through the paper and signed at the bottom of the page, then he reached for his wallet and produced his bank card which he inserted into the payment terminal Rachel was holding out.

Paperwork and payment complete, Rachel took the pink collar from Tom and asked the family to wait whilst she fetched Maisie.

Chapter Twenty Eight

Maisie had been having a sleepy day. She'd woken up the kennels that morning with a round of barking for breakfast, enjoyed a play in the exercise area with Elsie and finally she had returned to a clean bed and tidy kennel. She was just enjoying a snooze in the afternoon warmth when the door to the pen opened and in stepped Rachel, carrying a small, pink collar.

Elsie lazily opened one eye and surveyed the visitor but Maisie sat up and wagged her tail at the unexpected visitor. *This is different,* she thought, *different but OK*. She sat patiently as Rachel walked over and undid the kennel collar from around Maisie's neck then carefully placed the new pink collar with its heart shaped tally around Maisies throat.

Maisie was impressed. "Look how pretty I am!" she barked. Elsie ignored her, she knew Maisie enjoyed human attention.

Rachel smiled and picked up the tiny dog. "Come along, Maisie, you're going home now."

Maisie didn't understand the words, nor did she immediately realise that she was going away and would not see her friends again. She liked and trusted Rachel though and so she wagged her tail and sat still in Rachel's arms as she was carried out of the kennels.

Elsie watched her go then closed her eyes and continued her nap in the afternoon sun.

Rachel carried Maisie out of the kennels and across to the office. As she opened the door she felt the family's eyes focus on the small dog in her arms. She closed the door behind her back and gently put Maisie down on the floor.

Maisie had recognised Tom. She looked at the small human whose heart she had captured and shyly wagged her tail. Tom thought how well her new collar matched her dainty features. "How pretty she looks, Dad! I'm so glad Mum talked me into the pink collar, it really suits her." He smiled at his parents, who stood quietly whilst the tiny dog approached Tom and licked his hand as he bent down to stroke her.

Rachel was practical. "Do you have everything you need for her?" she said. "We have a well stocked shop if you need any more items."

"Goodness!" Tom's mum said, laughing. Remembering the shopping trips both online and in real life in preparation for bringing Maisie home, she added, "We've managed to get everything barring the kitchen sink, I think. I can't think of anything else one small dog could possibly need."

"Except..." Tom turned concerned eyes to his mum. "Except, she hasn't got a ball to play with. I know she likes to play ball, she was playing the first time I saw her." He reached inside his pocket and pulled out a five pound note. "I've got my pocket money, Mum. I've been saving it. Can I look for a ball for Maisie?"

Tom's mum was impressed with how her son was prepared to save and spend his own money on the dog, she nodded.

Rachel spoke to Tom. "Best pop into Reception then, they have a good selection of toys there. Do you have a lead for Maisie? Put it on her, then you can walk her over to choose yourself."

Tom nodded and looked at his mum who produced a matching pink lead and harness from her bag and gave it to Tom. Tom stooped down once more and, after a brief struggle to work out how it all fit together, managed to get the harness around Maisie's body and the lead clipped on. "We're ready to go!"

The family thanked Rachel for her help and left the office. Rachel watched as Maisie trotted happily after Tom, proudly showing off her new harness and nervous, yet excited to be going somewhere with these people. They popped into Reception where Tom and Maisie stood in front of a display stand with toys of all shapes and sizes displayed. Tom selected a small, yellow ball and held it out to Maisie. Gently, she took it from him, then dropped it on the floor and barked at him! Several people waiting in Reception turned round to see what the noise was.

"Plenty of time for play, Tom!" Dad laughed at the feisty Chihuahua, pleased to see the bond between his son and the dog deepening. "I think, for now, you should pay for the ball and we should get Maisie safely home. She can play when she's had time to settle. Let me hold her whilst you pay."

Tom agreed and handed the lead to his father. He went over to the lady at the desk and gave her his money. She smiled at him as she rang the amount up in the till and gave him some change which he counted carefully before putting the coins in his pocket. "Right Maisie, time to go home!"

Maisie was impressed with the morning's work so far. She liked Tom a lot, she felt safe with him. She'd been happy to have all the new collars and harnesses put on her, sniffing them cautiously at first then standing still whilst they were carefully adjusted so that they were snug but not too tight around her dainty neck and body. She had followed Tom gladly into Reception and had stared wide-eyed with him at the selection of toys until he had selected a ball which was just right for her small mouth. Her excited bark was supposed to start a game off but human words had been spoken and Tom had handed her lead to the larger human whilst he had gone up to the desk to pass something to the human there.

Now he was back, stroking her head and with that small ball hidden in his trouser pocket. She picked up on the word "home" and wagged her tail. *Where would today lead?* She wondered what was next and followed Tom and the other humans out of Reception.

Tom led her across the courtyard and out of a large gate into an area where there were lots of cars parked. Maisie's steps started to slow as she grew more nervous of leaving the kennels and her friends behind. Tom noticed her dragging her paws and encouraged her, "Come along, Maisie, it'll be alright. We're going home, but first you need to get in the car." He stooped down, pulled gently on the lead and the tiny Chihuahua looked up into his eyes. She decided that she would trust him and followed the gentle pull on her lead until they were standing at a big silver car.

Tom's dad opened one of the rear doors and held Maisie's lead whilst Tom climbed inside. Maisie looked up to see where Tom had climbed in but the step was far too large for her to jump up. She glanced at Tom's dad nervously until he placed both of his hands carefully around her body and picked her up and transferred her onto Tom's knee. Tom did up his own seatbelt and clipped a different seatbelt attachment onto Maisie. "There you go girl, you have your own seatbelt."

Both parents got into the front seats of the car and Dad started the engine. Maisie was quivering with excitement and a bit of trepidation, but Tom held her on his knee, spoke soothingly to her and soon they were underway. Maisie was so tiny she could not see much out of the windows but she got a sense of leaving everything she knew behind and starting a new adventure with Tom and his lovely family.

Back in the kennels, George had been walking with Jack and Norris around the exercise area where the three small dogs were being supervised by a human while they played. He had seen the little cream Chihuahua, all dressed up in her pretty pink harness, crossing the yard to the gate to outside, happy to be leaving with her new family. His heart had leapt to see her after all these weeks without seeing her in kennels, then it had sunk as he realised she was leaving with a new family and he would never see her again.

Jack, who had been chewing away at a dropped toy, noticed George standing and staring as the gate closed behind the family. "What's up, George? You look like you've seen a ghost?"

George continued to stare at the closed gate. "I think I have," he said sadly, "that was Maisie and she was leaving with a new family."

"Well, that's great for her, isn't it?" asked Jack. "She deserves a break, great girl Maisie."

George's whiskers drooped sadly, "I suppose so, she does deserve it." He remembered their night under the stars and sighed, "I do hope she'll be happy."

His reverie was interrupted as Norris came tanking up with a ball and dropped it at his feet. "Come on George, I've got a ball!" George half heartedly picked it up and dropped it again. "That's it," said Norris, "now catch me if you can!" He picked up the ball and started to run away.

"If I must." George trotted steadily after him, unaware that other human eyes were watching.

Rachel had walked over from the office to the kennels and had stopped to watch the small dogs playing in the exercise pen. She'd seen the gruff ginger dog with his whiskers bristling excitedly as he caught sight of Maisie leaving and then she had noticed how his body seemed to droop after she left. *So that's how the land lies,* she thought.

Chapter Twenty Nine

Life at the kennels carried on. Elsie was slightly surprised when her friend didn't return to the kennel by tea time, but she gratefully ate her meal on her own without the distractions of Maisie's barking. She exchanged small barks and grumbles with her neighbours on her late evening trundle around the outside run and the general consensus was that Maisie had got herself a fantastic new home and hopefully the others would get their new families soon.

In the morning there was no Maisie to start off the morning bark and although a few brave souls started to yap, without the impetus that Maisie had brought to it, it soon fizzled out. Over in the boys' kennels, George was sadder than ever as he missed hearing Maisie's small but determined bark in the morning.

But soon it was all go in the kennels. The steady stream of human viewings of the dogs now turned into a raft of departures. One by one the dogs were brought out of the kennels and taken across to the office where their pre-approved new owners cooed over them and took them away to start new lives.

First to go were Sue and Stu. An older couple with experience of the shaggy terriers wanted a pair to act as an alarm system for their large home and garden and arrived that afternoon to fetch them. They were more than happy to take both Cairns, pleased that the pair of siblings were already well bonded.

Next to be picked up was Max. He was adopted by a boisterous young family who admired his handsome looks and had plans to involve him in all their activities. He strutted proudly off with his new humans, glad to have been chosen early.

Likewise Ruby went with an adventurous family where she would be able to look after the young children and help them eat up food - as all Labradors enjoy doing.

Rogue was unexpectedly snapped up early by an elderly man who was coming to terms with losing his wife. The man felt that the old soldier could share country life with him with plenty of short walks and hunting of rabbits (if very slowly and with little chance of catching any). Then they could spend the evenings swapping war stories and memories of those they had lost. The match was perfect and Rogue and the man both left the kennels with a spring in their elderly steps.

Sidney, big and threatening in the overcrowded house, was transformed by a couple of weeks in kennels with proper supervision where he showed off his readiness to take commands when consistently given and good behaviour rewarded. A search conducted through the breed websites brought forward a man who had recently had to have his Doberman dog put to sleep due to its advanced cancer. He was thrilled to see Sidney up for adoption and, with a suitable home and breed experience, the adoption was agreed in a short time. Sidney and his new owner proudly left the kennels for their new life together.

The departures then slowed a little and daily life went on for the kennel dogs. Jack, who had already been reserved, wondered what the hold up was.

Molly, sitting at home, also wondered and picked up the phone. She was, apparently, still in the queue for a home check, but due to living slightly out of the area, this would be carried out by a partner organisation. Due to holiday leave, this had been delayed, but would soon be under way. Not to worry, Jack was still reserved and she could make preparations for his arrival. She called Joe and they decided to go shopping for things for Jack.

They chose to go to a big pet supermarket where Joe fetched a trolley so they could easily carry the items they needed. Molly decided on a grey dog bed for Jack to sleep in and a couple of matching bowls for his food and water. Joe pointed out a smart collar which was added to the trolley, together with a flexi lead and a harness in black. Molly had asked for details from Rachel as to the food Jack was being fed and she bought a bag of the recommended dry food. "I think that will do for now," she announced as she viewed the growing pile of items necessary for one small dog and wheeled the trolley to the checkout. She winced slightly at the amount added to her credit card, but decided she could afford it.

Meanwhile, Jack found himself without the company of his cousin as Norris was adopted by a young family, who were overjoyed at finding the small, playful dog. He, in turn, was overjoyed to have found a family where he could play all day, share the small children's biscuits when they forgot to watch him and, when tired, sleep with his head resting on the children's laps. Truly it was a fantastic match, but Jack was lonely when his friend left him behind with only an increasingly sad George to try to play with.

More of the boys were adopted. Titan was next to leave. The Staffie brightened up from his sulks when he was viewed by an active and fun family with teenage children. They loved his sense of fun and devil-may-care attitude to life and promised to offer him plenty of company and adventure. Titan left the kennels as quickly as his paws would take him, with never a look back to any of the dogs who had endured his misplaced reign of terror.

"I'm glad he's gone," Jack reported to nobody in particular. George was lost in his own sad world and simply sighed.

Toby, the excitable little golden spaniel, was adopted by a home working single mum of a teen daughter. Both these ladies clearly doted on him and he, in turn, was proud to go with him. He met

Jack in the exercise area before he went and promised him he would be good and try not to chase any posties, he really would try his very best to behave. Jack shrugged. *He probably won't behave,* he thought, *but that was part of Toby's charm.*

Betsy, the yappy little Yorkshire Terrier, was taken on by a deaf older lady, chuffed to find a little dog that not only would sit nicely on her knee, but would alert her to visitors at the door. Betsy was consequently spoiled rotten and revelled in her new role.

Finally, a family came in looking for a dog who could bond with their sensitive teenage daughter who had behavioural and learning difficulties. The cool aura exhibited by Elsie attracted them to the little Dachshund. Elsie intuitively understood that this sensitive human needed calm good sense, which she had in spades and the bonding was complete. Elsie left with them soon after, having formed a deep and healing friendship for life.

Meanwhile, the cats had not been seen since that fateful day back in the house, but it was rumoured that they had been given new homes. Jack truly didn't care as long as they weren't allowed to hurt him again.

This left just Jack and George from the house still waiting for new homes. George became increasingly morose as the days passed and his friends left the kennels. He didn't speak about Maisie, but Jack knew that he missed her. He could tell by the sad droop of George's moustache, the slow drag of his feet around the exercise pen and his lack of interest in any of the toys Jack tried to tempt him to play with.

Rachel noticed this too and was concerned about the small stand-offish dog. Whenever visitors came to see the dogs George lay in his bed or sulked at the back of the pen. Jack was welcoming as usual but as he was already reserved, visitors said hello to him, tried to avoid being licked by his long and penetrating tongue and ignored the silent George, passing by his kennel to look at the next one. *This won't do*, thought Rachel as she resolved to sort something out.

Chapter Thirty

Maisie had settled into her new home really well. The bond she had with Tom grew every day and she enjoyed the time she spent playing and walking with the family. Each night she settled down and slept in her new dog bed which Tom had insisted was placed at the foot of his bed, "Just so I can keep an eye on her." Tom's dad had agreed and put the soft bed in the required position, still pleased that the introduction of the small dog had brought Tom a little more out of his shell.

On the following weekend they had driven to a large area, covered with stones set in neat rows, many of which were adorned with flowers. Tom had explained it to Maisie in advance. "We're going to the cemetery, Maisie. We're going to see Grandad's grave." Maisie didn't know what he meant but had sensed his sadness and licked his face in sympathy.

At the cemetery, the family got out of the car and waited for Maisie to jump carefully out, then they walked quietly along the rows until they reached one plot in particular. "Here we are," said Tom, "Dad, have you got the flowers?"

Dad did indeed have the flowers. He produced a large, wrapped posy which Tom's mum took off him and worked some magic to place them neatly on the grave. Maisie looked on, she sensed the ritual of placing of the flowers and looking at the headstone hid a deeper loss and sadness and she clawed at Tom's leg, concern showing in her big brown eyes. "It's okay, girl, we're just making sure things are neat," said Tom, stroking her soft head.

The family stood quietly for a few moments, lost in their own thoughts, until Dad finally looked at Tom. "Time to go son?"

Tom nodded. "Bye Grandad, we'll be back again." He tugged gently on Maisie's lead and the family walked back to the car.

Back at the family home, Maisie had time to think. She sensed the sadness in Tom and somehow understood the loss of a great friend and influence in his life. She too had lost friends and remembered with fondness one in particular. Oh, how she missed the company of George with his twitching ginger moustache and silent, solid support. When she thought of him she felt quite down as she realised she would never see him again.

Over the next week Maisie lost a little of her sparkle, so much so that Tom noticed and wondered if she was unwell. He tried to tempt her with a game of catch but she half heartedly picked up the ball and then dropped it again. "What's up girl?" Tom asked, but Maisie couldn't make him understand so she just watched him with her huge brown eyes and gently sighed.

Tom asked his father if he thought Maisie was ill. Dad gently examined Maisie. The little dog seemed well enough, her skin and hair had healed well once the flea treatments given in kennels had worked and her appetite was still good. However, she seemed distracted and not as interested in her toys or playing with Tom. No, he didn't think she was unwell as such but he agreed with Tom that she seemed depressed. "Tell you what," he said to Tom, "I'll give Rachel a call and see if she can think of anything that might help."

Rachel was nonplussed when Tom's dad rang her. She remembered both Maisie and Tom with fondness and was sorry to hear Maisie was causing concern. "Tell you what," she offered, "why don't you bring her back to the kennels tomorrow afternoon? We have our visiting vet here and I can ask him to check her over as part of our aftercare service. I can also take a look at her myself to see if I can suggest anything."

Tom's dad was grateful for this offer and agreed to bring Maisie over with Tom after school the next day. Meanwhile, he told Tom to keep a close eye on Maisie and to tell him if she seemed to get any worse.

Maisie had a morose but comfortable evening with Tom, who sat with her after his meal and alternated between softly petting her and trying to tempt her with her toys. She half heartedly grabbed one toy but quickly put it down and settled back down into a sad doze on his knee.

The next day, Tom went to school, leaving a sad Maisie for a day at home with Mum who watched her whilst she worked at her computer. Dad promised he would pick him up promptly after school so they could take Maisie straight back to the kennels. "Don't forget, Dad, will you?" Tom's earnest entreaty was noted and Dad juggled a few more things in his busy diary to make sure he could be there.

At the end of school, Tom tumbled out of the school gates and met up at a fast run with his father who was waiting for him with a cautious Maisie, resplendent in her pink collar and matching harness and lead. "Hi Dad, hello Maisie!" Tom spoke excitedly and bent down to greet the tiny Chihuahua. Maisie wagged her tail in welcome and put both her paws on his knee so she could sniff and then lick her favourite human. Tom waved to some friends who were pointing at the sweet little dog he was patting and stroking. She danced along the pavement in her excitement to be at school. "This is Maisie," he said proudly, "my best friend!" Maisie's tiny chest seemed to puff up and expand with pride at being with Tom.

"Are you ready to go then?" asked Tom's dad and Tom nodded and took Maisie's lead from him before walking down the road to where the car was parked. Dad made sure they were all safely in the car then carefully eased the car out of the parking space and set off for the rescue centre.

Some minutes later they parked outside the centre and Tom unclipped Maisie from her seat belt, clipped her lead onto her harness and lifted her out of the car. He followed Dad into the centre and Maisie's eyes grew larger as she remembered where they were. She started to hang back a little, uncertain what this return meant. She had so enjoyed her time with Tom's family, and loved Tom with a passion, *But perhaps they didn't want a sad little dog after all?*

Tom noticed Maisie dragging behind and bent down to pick her up. "Don't worry, Maisie. We're just going to get you checked out, we're not going to leave you behind." Maisie didn't understand his words, but the soothing tone with which he spoke the words settled her and she loved being carried in his arms as she could lean into his warm body. She licked his face anxiously and tried to be brave and stop the trembling that had started to consume her small body.

Rachel had been looking out for the family and intercepted them as they approached the reception desk. "Hello Mr Jackson, hello Tom!" She looked at the trembling dog in Tom's arms. "Hello Maisie, too! Let's get her straight into the vet, he's in the examination room. If you would all follow me?" She led the way across the courtyard and into the long building where she knocked and then entered a small room.

By this time Maisie's fears had grown considerably. The small tremble had become uncontrollable and she cowered in Tom's arms. Rachel helped Tom to put the shaking dog onto the examination table, behind which a man stood. Maisie remembered him from before and she shrank towards Tom. "It's alright Maisie, I'm with you, nobody's going to hurt you." He spoke calmly to her and stroked her fur soothingly. Maisie gulped, closed her eyes and waited for the inevitable.

The vet spoke in a quiet but confident voice, he asked Tom and his father what the problem was and listened whilst they told him of the lethargy and depression exhibited by the tiny dog who, in a few weeks, had settled in so well with the family. He asked about her food and toilet habits and they confirmed they were normal. He then conducted a thorough examination of his patient, feeling his way around her body, checking for any pain or discomfort and checking her heart, eyes and ears with his scary vet instruments.

Maisie stood and trembled throughout the examination but didn't flinch or show any pain.

The vet scratched his head. "I don't know what to suggest. All her vital signs are normal and she doesn't seem to be in any pain." He turned to Rachel and asked, "Do we know much about her history?"

Rachel consulted her notes. "She was one of many dogs that were brought in from a single house. I think there was neglect but no abuse involved."

The vet thought for a moment. "Well we can't completely rule out a medical condition, but she's a young dog and she seems physically well. I suspect, however, it's psychological. It does take time for dogs to adapt when their surroundings change, even if for the better. She may be feeling the loss of her friends rather badly."

Tom was relieved that there was nothing physically wrong with Maisie, but he didn't understand why she missed her friends. "She's got me now, I'm her friend."

Dad put his hand on Tom's shoulder. "Of course she's got you, but she can still miss her other friends." He took a deep breath and continued, "It's like with Grandad, we all miss him every day. It hurts sometimes, even though we still have each other."

Tom nodded, he remembered the sense of loss and the sadness at losing his grandfather. His delight at owning the tiny and fun Chihuahua had helped heal his grief and make it less intense, but the sadness still resurfaced at times. As he remembered now, a faraway look crept into his eyes and the tiny dog recognised the look of sorrow and clawed at his arm with her tiny paw. Her dark eyes saw his sadness and, in that moment, they shared a deeper connection that brought comfort to both of them.

"I think she trusts you, Tom, let's see how she goes on with a little more time," Rachel said, then she thanked the vet and motioned for Tom to put Maisie down on the floor. She opened the door and let the family pass through and down the corridor to the end of the block. There, she hesitated, and instead of heading straight back across the courtyard to Reception, she beckoned them to follow her along the front of the row of kennels.

As they walked along the row, a cacophony of barking broke out and dogs lunged at the bars of the pens. Maisie shrank back in fear. These were new dogs, big dogs she didn't know and she was more frightened than ever that she was going to be abandoned back at the kennels.

Tom bent down and stroked her. "Come on Maisie, they can't hurt you, you're with me now." Maisie didn't understand what he said but she trusted Tom and gathered strength from his soothing words. Slowly, she walked on, keeping her eyes focussed only on Tom and trying valiantly to ignore the loud barks and yelps from behind the bars.

As they moved on, she thought she heard her name being called. "Maisie! Maisie, is it really you?" She looked up and saw a face she knew and heard a familiar voice, barking her name. "Maisie it's Jack!"

Chapter Thirty One

George was napping. He'd spent a lot of time asleep recently, he didn't like the hustle and bustle of the kennels and tried to zone out by sleeping. But his sleep was fretful. He dreamed of being back in the house and of the night under the stars with Maisie. Then he dreamt of being separated from her and unable to find her. He ran and ran and called for her and his paws shook and he made small barking noises in his sleep until Jack roused him and he woke up blinking blearily and remembered where he was.

That afternoon though, he was napping again. He vaguely heard the other dogs start to bark as some humans walked down the row of kennels, but he turned his head away and continued his snooze. As before, his dream returned but this time his lovely Maisie was being attacked by barking dogs. This time, his friend Jack had noticed her predicament and ran to her, calling out, "Maisie! Maisie, is it really you? Maisie, it's Jack!"

Then suddenly he was wide awake as a voice he knew and loved so well spoke. "Jack, yes it's Maisie! Jack, how lovely to see you again. Er..... is it just you?"

"Maisieeee!" Before Jack could answer, George jumped up, barking her name excitedly and rushed forward to the kennel bars, pushing his friend gently out of the way, his ginger moustache bristling with excitement.

"George! Oh George, I thought I would never see you again!" Maisie put her face against the kennel bars as George pressed his nose up close. She wagged her tail excitedly and pawed at the bars, trying to get closer to George.

Jack, excited to see a friend again, was especially pleased to see the change in his sad companion and decided to show his enjoyment by simply joining in with the general barking chaos in the kennels.

The small dog scenario had not been missed by the humans. Tom had been confused at first by the small, white fluffball of a dog who had attracted Maisie's attention by his intense and insistent barking. Then he was surprised when, instead of cowering, she turned and lunged towards the small dog. But this was nothing compared to her reaction when a small ginger dog came barrelling forward from his bed, barking loudly and shouldering his companion out of the way, causing her to jump forward, answering back. His Maisie had pressed her face up against the kennel bars, meeting the ginger dog's nose, almost in a kiss.

"Dad, Dad! Did you see that? Did you see that dog kiss Maisie?" Tom tugged at his father's shirt.

Dad laughed. He'd certainly seen the change in Maisie and how she'd perked up when she ran forward to meet the small ginger dog. He turned to Rachel. "She certainly seems to like that dog, do they know each other?"

Rachel nodded. "They came from the same house, along with the white one too. It does seem that she has a special bond with the ginger dog, look how they mirror each other." It was true. As Maisie pawed at the bars, so did George. When Maisie turned to look at Jack, George followed her gaze. When George pushed his nose through the bars, Maisie pressed her nose to his.

Tom looked on as Maisie and George continued in their special dance, mirroring each other's movements, wrapped up in the joy of their own world, oblivious to the watching humans. "It's like they're dancing!"

Just then a door clanged at the end of the kennel block and another lady approached. "Rachel, there's a visitor waiting at Reception for you. They've come to pick up a dog."

The interruption broke the spell of the moment and Maisie and George sprang apart as Rachel remembered her next appointment. "Of course, tell them I'll only be a minute whilst I show these people out."

As the other lady smiled and walked away to deliver the message, Rachel turned to Tom and his father. "I'll see you out now, let's see how Maisie gets on in the next few days." They walked slowly down to the end of the row of kennels with a shocked Maisie numbly following Tom. There, Rachel took her leave, turning back towards Reception and the family walked slowly on to the exit. From behind them they could hear the desperate barks of a small ginger dog. "Maisie! Maisieeee!"

Maisie was confused. It had been wonderful to see her friends once more and to see George looking so fine. It seemed as if her heart had missed a beat as he spoke her name and in all the excitement all she could say was, "George! Oh George!"

Now she was being ushered out of the kennels. Tom urged her to go forward with him by tugging on the lead and she followed, still mesmerised by the thought of George but not wanting to disappoint her favourite human. She definitely did not want to be left behind, she had formed a strong bond with Tom and wanted to go with him and to help soothe this little, lost boy. Besides, she remembered, she also rather enjoyed eating the little treats he gave her from his dinner plate when he thought his parents weren't looking. She heard George desperately calling her name from behind and hesitated, but she obediently followed Tom out of the kennels and back to the car, her steps slow and her tail and ears somewhat drooping.

That night, George paced up and down in his kennel, refusing to be calmed by the words of his friend. He was anxious. "My Maisie, she's gone again. Did you think she looked well, Jack? Those humans looked okay, but are they really looking after her? Why did they bring her back?" He paced and worried long into the night until he finally fell into an exhausted sleep beside Jack.

Similarly, at Maisie's home, there were worried words. Once Maisie had returned, the relief at seeing George again had worn off as she realised she'd never see him again. She was worried about him too. She thought he'd lost a little weight and his ginger moustache had seemed less bold and bristly somehow. She only ate a mouthful of her dinner and snoozed fretfully on Tom's knee that evening. Tom was concerned. "What's up, Maisie? Are you missing your friend?" Maisie simply closed her eyes and dreamed of a bristling ginger moustache and dancing under the stars.

Tom got ready for bed, still worried and concerned for Maisie. He tucked her up in her own bed with a favourite blanket for her to snuggle into and stroked her cream fur. "Night night Maisie, sleep tight, try not to worry about your friend." Maisie licked his hand.

Dad came in, made sure Tom was also safely tucked up in bed and watched as his eyes closed and his breathing settled into sleep. Maisie opened one eye as he quietly left the room. Now downstairs, Tom's parents were in earnest discussion. They talked long into the evening, trying to work out how they were going to settle Maisie and then finally, they had a plan.

Part Four - Finally Leaving

Chapter Thirty Two

"Breakfast!" Jack was already halfway over the pen, jumping with excitement. He delved his nose deeply into the bowl of dog food and hungrily snapped up a full mouthful of dog crunchies.

"Breakthfatht!" he shouted through the crunchies then carried them off to his bed where he tried once again to hide some. He was still confused where they were disappearing to each morning, especially since he took such care to hide them well. Just in case, he went back to the bowl and picked up a few more before chewing them thoughtfully. "Come on George! It's time to eat."

George was sad. He'd paced and worried all night long and now could barely open an eye. He sluggishly pulled himself out of his bed and half heartedly surveyed the food bowl before picking up and chewing a few crunchies.

"That's better," encouraged Jack, "now have a drink then you can eat a bit more." He nudged his companion towards the water bowl and watched him lap up some water. He could tell his friend's heart was broken, the ginger moustache was drooping and it seemed every step he took on those white paws was laboured. Jack didn't know how to console him and so he watched him chew a few crunchies and lie down on his bed once more.

After breakfast, the small dogs were once again taken to the large play area where Jack whizzed around and jumped on squeaky toys and George morosely sniffed in all the corners. Jack's favourite human, Rachel, came to watch the small dogs. "not long now, boys, exciting new homes for you," she told them.

George ignored her and Jack tried to climb on her knee and lick her. Rachel laughed and swiftly excused herself. "Paperwork to sort out!"

The boys were returned to their kennel which had been cleaned and tidied in their absence and yet again Jack wondered where his hidden crunchies had disappeared. George had no idea as usual and didn't seem at all interested in the mystery but Jack spent the next hour or so digging hopefully in his bed, trying to uncover where his treats had gone.

The day stretched out after that and the temperature grew warmer. Jack joined George in a snooze and the sounds of the hustle and bustle of the kennels receded as they slept deeper. Then there was the sound of the door to the kennel being opened and Rachel stepped into the pen, holding out a collar in her hands. Jack went up and licked her, George ignored her and tried to continue his snooze.

It was George, however, that Rachel wanted. She bent down to the sleeping dog and quietly stroked him. As he looked up at her she gently fastened the collar around his neck and attached a lead. "C'mon George, it's time to go. We've found you a home at last!"

George followed Rachel out of the kennel and lumbered slowly across the courtyard to the office. Inside the office, a smartly dressed lady was waiting. She bent down and offered her hand to him to sniff. "Hello George, nice to meet you." She nodded to Rachel who gathered up her paperwork, well satisfied with her day's efforts then held the office door open for the visitor and George to leave.

"Come on George, you're coming home with me!" The lady tugged gently on his lead and he followed her out of the gate and over to her waiting car. Once he hesitated, as she opened the car door for him, and looked back at the kennels, the last place where he had seen his darling Maisie. Then the lady pulled at the lead expectantly and he shrugged and jumped up into the car.

Chapter Thirty Three

Jack waited in the kennel for George to return and slowly the morning stretched on. He was snoozing when the door to the kennel opened. He looked up to see his favourite human, Rachel, approaching and wagged his tail. "Hello Jack," she spoke kindly as she bent down to him. She had a new collar in her hands and she slowly fastened it around his neck, removing the kennel's collar and tag as she did so. Jack licked her hand and gazed lovingly at her face. "Now Jack, it's time for you to go." She fastened on a lead and pulled gently for him to follow her out of the kennel.

They left the kennel block and crossed the courtyard to the office. Once inside the office, Jack saw two more humans who were vaguely familiar to him, an older lady who looked at him kindly and a younger man just behind. He wagged his tail slowly, but then hid behind Rachel's legs when one of the human's stepped forward. "Still a bit shy, Jack?" laughed Rachel, "here's your new owners, they've come to take you home."

"Hello Jack," said Molly. Jack shyly looked up at the lady and slowly wagged his tail. Rachel handed over the lead and Molly gently tugged on it, pulling the collar up around Jack's neck and causing the small dog to resist the pressure and pull back. Molly noticed Jack flinch and his eyes widen in panic as he felt the collar move on his neck. "I think we'd better find you a better harness," she said and looked at Rachel.

Rachel was pleased to see how Molly had already thought about the little dog's comfort and recognised his fears. *Great, he's getting a good home here,* she thought, but said out loud, "We have harnesses in our shop at Reception. If you'd like to choose one, I can help you find the right fit."

Molly bent down and let Jack sniff her hand. She gently picked up the small dog and held him close to her body. She could feel his little heart beating fast as he leant against her. "Don't worry, Jack, I've got hold of you now. I won't hurt you." Jack looked up at this new human, somehow he felt safe. He decided to trust her and so did what he was good at. He licked her face as Molly and Joe followed Rachel out of the office and into the reception next door.

In the little shop, they chose a soft but strong harness and carefully tried it on an anxious Jack. Having finally got his head and front paws through the harness, received a number of wet tongue licks then clipped the lead onto the new harness, Molly placed Jack onto the floor. "I think we're nearly ready!" she laughed as she fetched her card out to pay.

With Rachel having organised the last few bits of paperwork, finally they were ready to go. Molly stepped forward and pulled on the lead, Jack felt the harness tighten around his chest and felt confused. He sat down and looked up at Molly, who looked down at him. "Come on, Jack!" she said encouragingly, "There's a good boy now." She pulled again on the lead and slapped her hand quietly on her leg to encourage him forward. Rachel held the door open and Jack decided he would be brave after all and cautiously stood up and walked towards Molly. "Good doggie!" She smiled and stepped out of the door, Jack walked slowly after her and Joe followed with his hands full of dog treats, toys and food samples that they had bought in the shop.

They walked over to the gate and Jack could hear all the dogs in the kennels still barking, but as they passed through the gateway, the barking noises became quieter, until all he could hear was the footsteps of the two humans. They walked across the tarmac until they reached a blue car. Molly stopped and fumbled in the bag that was draped across her shoulder until she found a plastic item. She pressed a button on this and Jack jumped as the car made a "plip" noise and its lights flashed and locks unlocked. Molly opened one of the rear doors.

Jack sat down, quivering once more. He remembered the last time he'd been in a vehicle and how sick it had made him. Molly pulled once more on the lead and patted the car seat to try to encourage him to jump in. Jack squeezed his eyes shut, *Oh No!* He dug his little front paws into the ground and pulled back.

Molly was nonplussed. "Jack, you have to get in the car so we can take you home." She had another thought, "Joe, put those things in the boot and bring me the carrier."

Joe nodded and opened the boot of the car and spent a little time placing all the various items that a small dog needs in the boot, then lifted out a large black bag. As he brought it round to the side of the car and placed it on the ground, Jack could see that it was a bag with mesh panels on the side. Molly handed Jack's lead to Joe and carefully unzipped a panel on the top of the bag to reveal a soft mat inside. She gently reached down to Jack and picked him up. "Don't worry, Jack, I'm just going to pop you in the carrier, where you'll be safe." She put him inside the carrier and replaced his main lead with the internal lead to keep him fastened inside. She gave him a little stroke, told him he was a "good boy" and zipped up the panel. She picked up the whole carrier and positioned it in the car, attaching it to the seat belt so it wouldn't move. Jack lay in the carrier shivering with fright.

Molly motioned to Joe. "Perhaps you should sit in the back with him, he looks so frightened."

Joe nodded and got into the back seat of the car. He placed his hand on the top of the carrier and spoke quietly to the quaking dog. "Don't be scared, we're taking you home." Jack licked his lips nervously but continued to shake.

Molly got into the driver's seat "We'll get going and not prolong the journey." She started the engine and eased the car out of the parking space.

Jack closed his eyes as the car moved forward, *Oh dear I feel queasy...*

Molly drove the car carefully, speeding up and slowing down gently, and taking corners very slowly so that the movement of the car was minimised and Jack would be comfortable. However, despite her best efforts, by the time they reached the motorway, Jack had been sick. Joe spoke kindly to the distressed dog and tried to keep him calm, but Jack sat in the vomit and dribbled anxiously over himself.

Molly reached her exit on the motorway and the car slowed, she drove carefully along a few more streets until finally she turned into a smaller road where she turned off the road and parked up on a driveway in front of a smart semi detached house. "Here we are, now let's sort you out." She got out of the car and opened the rear door where she studied the carrier. Jack quivered silently in his mess as Joe helped to unbuckle the carrier and pass it out to Molly.

"I think it will be best if we take him through to the garden," said Molly, "will you open the doors for me?" She could see they would need to clean the little dog up, but in view of the warm weather didn't think she needed to risk the mess on her carpets just yet. So Joe went ahead of her, unlocking and opening the doors to the house and into the garden at the back. Once outside, she set the carrier on the lawn and asked Joe to fetch a bowl of warm water, a sponge and a towel and to bring Jack's flexi lead.

Jack sat in the carrier, trying to get his bearings. He shivered despite the warm day as the vomit and slobber soaked through his fine hair. Slowly the world seemed to settle and he scratched the front of the carrier to attract Molly's attention. "Let me out!" he barked, "Let me out of this thing!"

Joe returned from the house with a handful of things as requested. "Woof!" he heard, "Woof woof!"

He put the items down next to Molly and spoke to Jack, "There, there now. Won't be long."

Now they were ready, Molly unzipped the top of the carrier and clipped the lead onto Jack's harness. "Come now, little one," she soothed as she picked the tiny dog up and put him down on the grass. Next she took the sponge and carefully wiped Jack down until he was clean and then used the towel to dry him off. Still damp but feeling slightly brighter, Jack tried to climb on her knee and put his tongue out to lick her. Molly was quicker though and held him off, laughing, "Oh no you don't! You need to settle a bit first."

Chapter Thirty Four

Jack sat on the grass and felt the warm sun on his back. Nervously, he sniffed his surroundings. Outside! He'd never really been outside before and certainly not to an outside like this. Back at the hoarder's house the Bigs had told tales about how dangerous the outside was and scared all the smaller dogs into never setting foot out of the house. Outside was where the cats went and fought with other cats and where mad dogs like Toby who ignored the rules went to chase Postie. Outside was where the monsters lived. He quivered and tried once more to climb on this nice human's knee for safety but she laughed and pushed him gently off.

He looked down at the grass. He'd never seen grass in his life before, this wasn't like the torn up and stained flooring he was used to. He sniffed it cautiously. It smelt of earth and greenery goodness. He took a couple of small steps across the grass, listening for any monsters as he went and stopped to sniff once more.

Molly sat patiently and let the small dog explore. Jack kept looking at her to check she wasn't going to leave him and made his way a few feet across the lawn to where Joe was sitting. Jack sat down beside him and raised a paw to claw at his leg. Joe smiled, "Hello Jack. Are you feeling better?" Jack took this as encouragement and tried to climb on Joe's knee, but Joe was quicker and held him off with one hand. Jack promptly licked it, then turned to look at Molly. She was still sitting in the sun, seemingly without a care in the world. Jack decided this place must be safe after all, at least whilst Molly was there.

The humans sat in the sun and watched as the small dog sniffed and snuffled around the garden. Fortunately, Molly had had the sense to put him on a flexible lead and so he could safely go exploring without her having to follow him too closely. First, he sniffed his way around the lawn. It was made up of fragrant, green grass with other small plants he'd never met before all mixed in. Every so often he would come across a small mound of soil that had been pushed up from below. He didn't know what worm casts were, but he licked them just in case. They tasted, well, sort of earthy, but no monsters came out of them and so he moved on.

He walked on across the grass, away from the humans, until he came to a stretch of pebbles surrounding a large oval area. He heard a gushing sound and noticed there was water falling over a rocky bank behind and tumbling into the oval area which he now recognised as a pool of water. He edged cautiously forward and put his nose into the water. It was cool and he put out his long tongue and lapped it slowly. Jack closed his eyes and breathed out slowly, *This is lovely,* he thought and pondered if this place was, perhaps the place the dogs had spoken about, Nirvana.

His daydream didn't last long. An enormous mouth surfaced just an inch away from his nose and gulped in the air. "Aaaargh!" Jack screeched and leaped backwards, "Monsters!" He glared at the water and saw a dark shape swimming below the surface. "Monsters in the water!

Behind him he could hear Molly laughing softly as she reeled his lead in a little and got up to come over to him. "Oh Jack, watch out for the fish in the pond," she spoke quietly but reassuringly, "they won't hurt you but they may splash you."

As Molly sat down beside him, she reached out and stroked him on the neck. Feeling her reassuring touch, Jack calmed down. He crawled onto her lap and gave her face an adoring lick. From the safety of her knee he turned back to the pond and looked into the dark water. He could see more of the dark shapes, swimming below the surface. Molly had called them fish and laughed. *Perhaps they aren't monsters,* he mused.

As he watched, once again a pair of large lips broke the surface and gulped in the air. "Feeed me pleeease," the fish gasped. Joe came up behind them. In his hand he held a plastic tub with small pellets of some kind of food in them. As he came closer to the pond, the other dark shapes in the pond sensed his approach and they too started to push their lips up and gasp in the air, "Feeed us! Feeeed us now!"

Joe threw some of the pellets on top of the water and the fish went crazy. They leapt and thrashed around the pond, flapping their fins and tails so they could gobble up the food. Jack shrank back but felt Molly's hand on his back, comforting him and so he watched in amazement as these dark shapes ate their fill and slowly sank back down to the deeper recesses of the pond. Soon the surface of the water was still again, barring the splash of the waterfall tinkling steadily into the pond. Jack stretched and got off Molly's knee. He noticed that one of the pellets had fallen onto the pebbles at his feet. He sniffed it, decided it smelled good, gobbled it up and stood wagging his tail at the two humans. Molly and Joe giggled.

The rest of the day was filled with more settling in. Having explored the garden, Jack was led into the house and introduced to the rooms downstairs. There was a hot conservatory with a dining table and chairs set beneath glazed window panels that allowed views over the slabbed patio. Jack saw his reflection in the patio doors and thought it was another dog, he bared his teeth and growled, but Molly called him away and led him into the kitchen.

The kitchen was full of interesting food smells and Molly showed him one corner where two bowls sat on the floor. One was full of clean water and the other had a couple of dog crunchies in it. "That's your food and water, just a little snack for now." Molly watched as Jack wolfed down the crunchies and gave a cursory sniff at the water.

Next was the living room and Jack was impressed. A soft beige carpet covered the floor and there were two large brown leather settees for sitting on. Molly knelt down and removed his harness and lead. "You can explore for yourself now, but no going up the stairs," she told him. Jack simply licked her hand and tried to get on her knee, but she pushed him off and waved him away. Jack sat down and looked at her until she got up and went into a small hallway to hang up the lead. He followed, more beige carpet and a front door. He knew about front doors, they led outside where the scary monsters lived and he shuddered and quickly scampered back to the living room where Molly and Joe had sat down, one on each of the two settees.

Jack scratched again at Molly's leg and was once more waved away so he sniffed his way around the floor, anxiously watched by two pairs of human eyes and then went back and sat down in front of Molly. Molly waved her hand towards a dog bed set down in front of the settee. "Jack, why don't you settle down? There, lie down on that bed."

Jack didn't understand though, he looked up at Molly and scratched at her leg, *I just want to lie on your knee.* Molly waved him away once more.

Jack sat for a little while, hopefully looking up at Molly, then suddenly closed one eye. It was only a quick blink, but Molly saw it. "He winked at me!" Jack sat immobile staring up at her with his big, brown, bulgy eyes. Molly bent down and stroked the small dog, he licked her hand. "Whatever will we do with you?" she laughed.

The rest of the day passed slowly. Jack was tired, so very tired after his exciting day but he kept himself awake, keeping watch over everything these new humans did. When Molly went into the kitchen to prepare food he followed her and stood right behind where she was standing. Whenever she stepped back he had to move quickly to prevent her from stepping on him, but still he persisted, a quiet little shadow watching her work and following her eagerly.

The humans ate their dinner in the glass sided room they called the conservatory with the doors flung wide open to the garden. Although Jack was free to go out he stayed at Molly's feet, waiting for her to finish her dinner then followed her back into the kitchen and watched silently whilst she stacked the dishwasher.

After their meal, the humans took Jack into the garden once more, but this time Molly had a different idea. She had brought the couple of toys she'd purchased at the kennels and she tried to attract Jack's attention with them. Jack danced along, eager to see what she had in her hand and forgetting the horrors of the garden. First Molly tried a ball which, although Jack chased it the first time she threw it, he didn't manage to get his small mouth around and so rapidly lost interest. Then Molly tried a small rubber bone, again Jack chased it, but lost interest once he caught up with it. Joe picked it up and tried to tempt Jack with it, but Jack preferred to sniff the grass to check if any worms were around.

Molly gave up. "I don't think he's a toy sort of dog." The games over, Molly returned to the kitchen where she put a couple of tasty dog biscuits in his bowl and watched quietly as he removed them and took them away into the hall to eat. There didn't seem to be any other dogs to take his food off him here, but Jack thought it best to be safe.

The humans spent the evening in the living room, looking at a square shaped object in the corner from which sounds came and on which colourful pictures moved. The humans called this thing the television and laughed and chatted as it showed its funny pictures.

Periodically, Molly would get up and walk into the garden, calling for Jack to follow. This he did slavishly, but with no interesting toys, he had to be persuaded to step onto the grass each time, he preferred the solid ground of the path. *No worms there.*

Molly stood with him as he sniffed around and scratched at her leg. "Do wee wee!" she trilled in a high voice, but Jack didn't understand so just licked her leg instead.

After a few minutes, Molly decided nothing was happening, so returned to the house and the television with Jack scooting quickly after her. *Don't leave me out here!*

Jack was extremely tired by now, but he continued to sit in front of Molly, watching her with drooping eyes. He couldn't settle, he just wanted to sit on her lap. Finally, after yet another unproductive round in the garden, Molly decided it was bed time. She didn't want to take any chances of him having an accident on her clean carpets so she took him through into the kitchen where she had moved the small dog bed, putting it in one corner. She'd also left out a small, square sheet nearby, something she called a puppy pad. She picked Jack up and placed him in the dog bed whereupon he swiftly left it. She tried again, and then again and finally gave up as Jack followed her to the door. She had a little worry at this point that he'd sit on the hard floor all night and so placed a small towel next to the door, then swiftly turned to Jack and sat him on the towel. *Perhaps this would do.*

Jack watched as Molly turned off the light and plunged the kitchen into darkness as she stepped through the doorway and closed the door behind her. He scratched at the door and whimpered, "Don't leave me!" He heard her as she hesitated on the other side, then her footsteps receded and he was alone. He heard the creak of the stairs in the house and Molly and Joe saying goodnight to each other and then all went quiet. He anxiously scratched at the door a few more times, but tiredness finally caught up with him and he curled up on the towel next to the door where he'd last seen Molly and fell into an exhausted sleep.

Chapter Thirty Five

Whilst Jack had been getting used to his new home, George had arrived at his. The lady had driven home carefully and George had unexpectedly enjoyed the journey, his whiskers twitching as he took in new sights and smells. His heart still ached for Maisie but out here there was life!

The car drew up outside a smart house and the lady got out. She reached into her handbag and brought out a mobile phone into which she started to talk. "Yes, we're just outside now. Can you distract them for a minute? Yes, the garden may do it."

George was puzzled, but he sat patiently wagging his tail until the lady let him out of the car and followed her to the front door of the house. They stepped into the cool hall and George caught a faint smell on the air. He dropped his nose and started sniffing the floor. *Was it… could it be?*

But the lady calmly, yet insistently, tugged on his lead and made him follow her through the house until they reached the open back door where she removed the lead and let him stand and look out. He stood on the step and watched as he saw a small boy, playing fetch with a tiny cream dog who ran after a small ball whilst a man he judged to be the father laughed at her valiant efforts to evade capture once she caught it. The three were wrapped up in their game, with only the father noticing the new arrival, but George gasped at what he saw, "Maisie!"

Maisie had been having a quiet and morose morning yet again. She'd been sleeping in the kitchen and hadn't heard the car pull up outside the house. Deep in her own world, she'd ignored the sound of the mobile phone going off and the quick conversation between Dad and the caller. She'd reluctantly allowed herself to be woken and chivvied out into the garden along with Tom and the words "Let's go play a game" echoing in her tiny ears. For Tom's sake she'd joined in the game as her antics made him laugh and she loved to see the smile come out on his serious little face.

And so she was playing a game of fetch with Tom and he and his father were laughing when she caught the gasp of her name. At first she thought she was mistaken, but the voice repeated her name, a bit louder this time. "Maisie!"

She dropped the ball and turned to look and saw a small ginger dog standing on the step with his moustache bristling excitedly. "George!" She couldn't believe her eyes, her kind, brave George was here!

Tom watched as the two dogs stared at each other, then slowly Maisie stepped forward and walked up to George. George was transfixed, staring at Maisie as she crossed the garden. Maisie reached him and stretched up to sniff him, then let out a little bark. This broke the tension and the two dogs sniffed each other then licked each other's ears and faces, before Maisie quickly nipped George on the shoulder and set off around the garden at a fast gallop. Not to be outdone, George followed, but at a more sedate pace as he didn't really know the garden. The two dogs raced and played excitedly as Tom looked on, wide-eyed.

Tom's dad walked up and put his hand on his son's shoulder and Tom looked up at him, smiling. "Mum went back for the other dog, Dad?" His Dad nodded. "Yes she did. Rachel thought it would be good for both of them since they have such a strong bond and I have to say I think she's right."

Tom's mum came up and slipped her hand into Dad's free hand. "Just look at them! They're dancing."

It was true, George and Maisie had found each other again and the stand-offish bristling ginger dog was leading the tiny, pretty cream one in a series of steps and twirls around the lawn. Breathless from her exertions, Maisie finally stopped. "Oh George, it really is you!" she panted.

George ceased his dancing and looked at Maisie, a little shyly now. "Yes, I'm here. I, er, I missed you, you know."

"I missed you too. I thought I'd never see you again!" Maisie was wistful now. "But my lovely humans have brought you to me."

George remembered the humans. "Perhaps you'd better introduce me," he told her.

Maisie led George up to where Tom, Mum and Dad were standing and both dogs waited with gently wagging tails whilst Tom knelt down and slowly stroked them. Maisie closed her eyes as she felt Tom's fingers caressing her skin, *Ooh that felt good!* George, a bit reticent at first, eventually gave in and surrendered to the good sensations of Tom's stroking on his fur and closed his eyes too.

"Why, look at that!" Mum observed. "Two happy little doggies! We must have done the right thing. Thank goodness we went back for George, they look so content together with Tom."

It was true. A happiness and contentedness stole over the entire family in the next few hours and days. George's gruff and stern demeanour melted whenever he saw Maisie and his playful side came out. His calmness infected everyone he came into contact with and soon, not only Maisie, but the entire family were under his spell.

Tom tried to understand why, George reminded him of something, or perhaps it was someone? Later that evening, as he was getting ready for bed, the two dogs following him and silently watching him clean his teeth and put his pyjamas on, it came to him. He was reviewing the events of his day with Dad and told him he thought how much his grandad would have laughed at the two dogs and how pleased he would be to see Tom taking care of them. "That's it! He reminds me of Grandad! There's an old sort of wisdom about him, it's just like Grandad."

Dad agreed, "I see what you mean, he seems calm yet knowing. I think we're all going to benefit from George in our lives."

George, of course, was oblivious to these musings, but he knew several important things. Firstly, he'd found his Maisie and he was going to love and protect her. Secondly, he'd found a lovely family with whom he felt he belonged and had already fallen slavishly in love with Tom's finger scratches.

Maisie was happy too. Gone was the sadness in her eyes and the morose expression on her pretty face. She knew that her George was here with her, stoically helping her face any challenge life would throw at her. Furthermore, George had the same effect on Tom and his family. Maisie had heard Dad describe him as an "old soul" and whilst she didn't understand the meaning of the words she got the drift of them, it felt like George belonged there.

At night, the two little dogs settled down to sleep together in the dog bed at the foot of Tom's bed, Maisie just keeping one ear up to check Tom was alright. Once Tom had fallen asleep, there was just the sound of regular breathing as they dreamed of happy trips to fields and woods and dancing under a moonlit sky.

Chapter Thirty Six

Jack had a fretful night. Exhausted, at first he fell into a deep sleep, but as the night wore on, he started to feel the hardness of the floor beneath the towel he was curled up on and he tossed and turned to get more comfortable. He dreamed. He was in a tunnel with cats chasing him and trying to catch him with their huge claws. As he tried to reach the light at the end, they caught up with him and they turned into huge gulping monsters that threatened to engulf him. He tried to escape and his paws twitched as he ran and he cried out as a large trap door swung shut at the end of the tunnel and he was trapped.

"Jack, wake up!" Molly had opened the door to the kitchen to find him scrabbling at the door, his eyes wild and a whimpering coming from his mouth. She bent down to hold him softly whilst he came to.

"Whaa...at?" Jack was confused and sat blinking at Molly in the dawn light. He recognised her and felt her calm assurance.

"Wake up sleepy head, I think you were dreaming." Molly stroked the small dog, noting how his nice new dog bed remained undisturbed and the towel by the door showed signs of the struggle he'd had through the night. "Never mind, I'm here now, time to let you out."

She picked up the unloved dog bed and put it in the living room then went back through the kitchen and over to the door that led out and opened it. Jack followed her eagerly, walking almost under her feet as he tried to keep up with her and went through the attached conservatory, standing by her feet as she opened the door into the garden. "Out you go." Jack stood and stared up at her and wagged his tail. "You need to go out." More tail wagging and Jack helpfully licked Molly's ankle. "Oh dear, of course this is going to take some time."

Molly, still fresh from bed with dishevelled hair and dressed in her fetching pink dressing gown and matching slippers, fervently hoped none of her neighbours would be looking out from an upstairs window at just that moment and stepped out onto the patio. Jack followed her and stood looking up at her once more. Molly walked across the patio and up a small step and stood on the garden path, quickly checking the neighbours' windows. All the curtains were closed, she felt relieved.

Jack, as before, followed her and stood on the path beside her. "Oh dearie me, well here goes." Molly stepped onto the dew covered grass and clicked her tongue, "here Jack." Jack finally got the message and gingerly stepped onto the grass. It took several minutes and plenty of encouragement before he finally relieved himself. "Good boy, Jack!" Molly was so pleased as she was getting a bit cool and her pink slippers were starting to look rather damp. She cast one last glance at the neighbours' windows, turned and headed back into the house, Jack skipping to keep up.

Molly reached the kitchen and filled up the kettle. "Time for some coffee, then we'll work out our day." She pottered around the kitchen, putting various things in a large mug whilst she waited for the kettle to boil. Jack sat and watched her, he was happy to see this human, already he had warmed to her and felt safe.

The coffee made, Molly took it into the living room and put it on a side table whilst she sat down on the settee. Jack followed and pawed at her leg hopefully. *Let me up, I only want to sit on your knee.*

Molly shooed him gently. "No, Jack, you mustn't get on my furniture, there's a nice soft bed for you on the floor." She was determined that this dog would not be allowed on her nice settee but it was going to be hard resisting Jack's little face. He sat in front of her, as on the previous evening, with large brown eyes, watching her steadily. Then, he did it again, one eye closed. Molly saw it and laughed. "Wink at me all you like, I've made up my mind. Dogs are not allowed on the settee."

Molly finished her coffee and got up. "Now, I'd better make you and I some breakfast." She walked through to the kitchen and started to put some dog food into Jack's bowl. She followed the instructions that Rachel had given her, using the same type of food, as she didn't want to upset Jack's digestive system. She mixed a small amount of meat in with some of his favourite crunchies and put the bowl down on the floor.

Jack sniffed the bowl hungrily, it smelt good. He gulped down the dog meat at once, barely stopping to chew. *Mmmm that tasted good!* He surveyed the crunchies and carefully picked up as many as he could fit into his mouth and took them out of the kitchen and into the living room. Here, he wandered around, poking into the corners of the room and scratching at the carpet. Occasionally, he'd set the crunchies down and eat one, but then he'd pick up the rest and repeat his scratching and scraping in the corners.

Molly smiled. "I won't take them off you, you know, but if you want to hide them, go right ahead." So, Jack ate some crunchies, hid some and went back for more from his bowl until it was completely empty. Molly, meanwhile, filled a bowl with some cereal and fruit and ate her own breakfast.

Joe came downstairs and poured himself a glass of orange juice. Jack shyly wagged his tail in greeting, then continued his game with his food. Joe looked at Molly with a slightly amused expression on his face. "I see he's trying to hide breakfast." Molly explained that she thought it was because he'd been kept with other dogs and was so small he wanted to keep his food hidden. Joe agreed. "That makes some sense, yes. But it is quite comical, how he moves them around, then eats them anyway."

That was true, within half an hour, it seemed that Jack had eaten all his crunchies and decided to go for a little exploration of his own, sniffing his way around all the corners of the living room in case any crunchies remained hidden.

The day passed in a similar vein to the one before, with Jack exploring the house and garden and getting used to his new humans. He learned some new boundaries by trial and error, even though he was unimpressed by some of them. Apparently, as well as not being allowed on the furniture, Molly did not approve of him going upstairs, nor did she appreciate it when he decided to relieve himself on the landing carpet. These little mistakes were met with a firm "No, Jack!"

He watched sheepishly as Molly, with a look of deep disapproval on her face, carried a bucket of warm water upstairs and started scrubbing at the carpet. After that episode, he was placed under more careful surveillance with half hourly, accompanied trips into the garden.

Later in the day, Joe went out of the front door of the house and returned some time later with something exciting in a shopping bag. Jack followed him as he took the bag into the kitchen and put the bag on the worktop where Molly and he unpacked it together. Jack could only hear various rustlings as he was far too small to see what was going on, but he heard Molly laugh as she seemed to approve of what Joe had bought. Molly took a pair of scissors out of the kitchen drawer and snipped a tag off whatever they were both looking at. Then she carried it into the living room and knelt down on the floor and held out her hand to Jack.

Jack had followed, partly because he was quickly falling in love with this human who fed him and looked after him, and partly because he was curious and interested in what she had in her hand. He looked shyly at what she was holding out to him. It was a small, yellow stuffed toy with a brown furry tail. He reached up to her outstretched hand and sniffed the toy. "Good boy, it's a squirrel, you know. A yellow squirrel for you to play with." Jack didn't understand all the words but the tone was encouraging and the word "good" seemed to indicate he was doing something right.

He waited until she put the toy on the floor, then he sniffed it again. He decided it looked a little bit like his favourite sock and picked it up. *Oh joy!* He felt the soft material in his mouth and instinctively bit down on it. The toy screamed and Jack dropped it and jumped back, startled.

Molly giggled. "It's got a squeak inside, Jack. Try again." Jack couldn't resist and he approached the toy cautiously and picked it up again. This time he was prepared for the squirrel to make the noise and as he bit down he did so more carefully and didn't provoke such an indignant squeak. "That's better," crooned Molly, "now let's see if we can play," and she took hold of the furry tail that drooped out of Jack's mouth and gave it a tug.

This is fantastic! Jack pulled back with all his might and entered into a spirited tug of war with Molly. He dug his little paws into the carpet and pulled and pulled. Molly pulled in the other direction, letting the tiny dog occasionally make a bit of ground and finally letting go of the toy, much to Jack's delight. Jack then ran off into the hall where he dropped the toy on the doormat then lay down and proceeded to chew it.

Molly heard a motley noise of chewing and squeaking coming from the hall and turned to Joe, smiling. "Well, that seems to have done the trick. He likes small furry toys, we'll have to keep a look out for some more."

The squeaky toy came in handy during Molly's regular trips out to the garden. Jack had been reluctant to go out and even more resistant to the idea of standing on the grass and Molly had started to run out of ideas to tempt him. But the squeaky toy solved all of that. Molly found that if she picked it up and took it outside, then Jack would follow, squeaking himself and excitedly dancing on his hind feet. In this way, she developed a better way of making sure Jack knew to go in the garden and made it into a fun game at the same time. She still had to accompany him and his toy friend, but she felt that a small gaggle on the lawn was a small price to pay for clean carpets.

It was on one such occasion that Jack, after he'd danced out into the garden and once he'd sniffed and peed on the lawn, decided to explore the garden further. Molly had decided that, in view of it being a hot summer's day, she would lie back on a chair on the patio and daydream a little. She was aware of Jack wandering off, but she knew the garden was enclosed and that he'd been shown all around it several times, so she was happy that the little dog was getting braver. Rachel had warned her she would need to introduce things slowly so as not to overwhelm the tiny dog, which was the reason he hadn't been out for a walk yet. *A couple of days to get his bearings, that was what was needed.* Molly smiled and closed her eyes in the warm sun.

Jack was enjoying playing in the sun. He'd taken his squirrel out onto the lawn and had practised pouncing on him and shaking him violently. Squirrel had squeaked in protest but this had made Jack more excitable and the playing got a bit rougher for a time. Finally, Jack got a bit bored and looked up. Molly was snoozing in a chair, her eyes closed and mouth slightly open, Jack was satisfied his human helper was at hand. He started to walk down the garden just as a large, fat bird landed at the edge of the pond. *A bird! In my garden!* Jack had already become territorial and dashed forward as fast as his little legs would carry him towards the bird, growling under his breath, "Grrrr!" The bird took off quickly but landed again on the fence by the pond but out of reach of the small dog.

"Grrrr!" muttered Jack once more at the bird.

"Coo, coo!" tweeted the bird back, fluffing its feathers out and glaring at the interloper.

The two stood and glared at each other for a minute, then Jack started to giggle. The bird looked down its beak indignantly. "Coo, coo! What are you laughing at? It's not funny making a pigeon flap."

Jack looked at the rather ungainly bird, standing on the fence, fluffed up in its indignance. He walked closer to inspect it and looked up. "Oh! Is that what you are then? A pigeon? Is that a special type of fat bird?"

The pigeon ruffled its feathers up even more. "Fat bird! Well, of all the...." It glared at Jack. "Yes I'm a pigeon, but there's nothing fat about me. Just what did you think you were doing, giving me a fright like that?"

Jack broke into his most winning smile, "I'm sorry, I didn't mean to upset you. I didn't realise you were an erm... an un-fat pigeon. I'm Jack by the way, pleased to meet you umm..."

The pigeon was slightly mollified by Jack's apology. "The name's Bertha." She paused and narrowed her eyes as if reading Jack's mind. "Now, no jokes about my size again, or we'll be falling out." She strutted along the fence to get a better view of Jack. "What are you? Some sort of dog?" She peered closer still. "You're not very big are you?"

Jack agreed that yes he was a dog and no he wasn't a very big one at all. Bertha continued to make observations about his lack of stature and the general dishevelled state of him, which Jack felt was unfair and told her so. "Well, just look at your ears, why you can't even prick one of them properly," countered Bertha.

This was true but something which Jack didn't really want to be reminded of as the small scar at the base of his ear attested to his traumatic argument with the cats. "Cats," he said mournfully, "cats did it."

Bertha's attitude changed and she looked more sympathetically at him. "Oh, cats! The stories I could tell you about ca...."

Then she was gone. A quick flap and all that was left was a feather floating in the breeze and a black shadow making its way along the fence to where Bertha had been sitting a moment before. Jack saw the shadow and his ear throbbed at the memory. *Cats!*

He didn't wait to find out any more, he leapt backwards towards the safety of the patio and Molly, backwards onto some green leaves. *Must escape!* But then he was falling, falling through water and the water was filling his mouth and nose and his ears. "Brffggle!" he tried to scream, but the water filled his mouth and his cry for help was quenched. He struggled in the water, aware of dark moving shapes bumping into his legs and gliding away. *Monsters!* In his terror he swallowed some of the dark, pond water and scrambled harder as he went under the water's surface again and all he could see was blackness.

And then he heard Molly calling his name, "Jack! Jack, I'm coming!" He made one more massive effort to struggle towards her voice and suddenly his legs were touching solid ground and his paws were dragging his heaving body out over the pond bank. He hauled his hind legs out and sat, coughing and panting, beside the pond just as Molly reached him.

Molly, who had been dozing in the sun, had heard the kerfuffle at the pond and opened her eyes to see a small white object struggling in the water. Scanning the garden for Jack, she had realised immediately that Jack had fallen in and leapt to her feet. She'd run up the path, calling his name, only to reach the pond as he pulled himself out. He now stood on the bank of the pond, coughing, with his sides heaving and glaring at the dark water. "Oh Jack, are you alright?" She touched the now trembling dog on his side. "Oh dear, think I'd better get you sorted out." She pulled him closer and sniffed him, he smelt of fishy pond water, but was starting to breathe more easily. "I think, perhaps a bath's in order, though. Better come with me."

She picked him up and carried him onto the house, calling for Joe to fetch towels and something called "the dog shampoo". She carried him up the forbidden stairs and into the bathroom where she plonked him in a large white bath. Jack shuddered and tried to climb out but Molly held him firmly whilst she showered and shampooed the pond water out of his fur. She gently massaged his skin which was still tender from his scratching even though the fleas that had caused the itchiness were now dead and gone. She gently washed off the shampoo and kept it out of his eyes and ears but still Jack shook and shivered. Then she was finished and she turned off the shower and picked Jack up and placed him on the bathroom floor where she laughed as he shook and covered her with water, then she towelled him off and finally let him go.

Jack did a quick sweep of the upstairs, trotting quickly into Molly's neat pink and grey bedroom where he inhaled her scent. Upon her call he came darting out and ran down the stairs as fast as his tiny legs could go whilst Molly tidied up the bathroom behind him, gathering up the dog washing kit and towels before following him downstairs.

It was lucky it was a warm day, for Jack shivered a bit from his damp fur. Molly wrapped him up in another towel and sat on the floor with him for a little while whilst he dried out. Jack looked up at her and licked her face adoringly as she told Joe the tale of Jack's scrape with danger in the pond. Joe, seeing that Jack was unharmed, seemed unimpressed with his antics and wanted to know if his fish were alright. Molly assured him that she thought they were. Jack considered this and concluded that the fish monsters were fine, which was more than he could say for himself as he was starting to feel just a little bit queasy.

Chapter Thirty Seven

The afternoon was over by now and all the excitement of his adventures in the pond and having a bath had made Jack quite tired. When Molly made herself a cup of coffee and sat down, Jack clawed at her leg once more and gazed up adoringly at her with his huge brown eyes. "No Jack," said Molly firmly, "dogs are still not allowed on furniture." She patted him and motioned towards where his soft bed sat. "Go in your bed, Jack." Jack ignored this and continued to sit in front of her on the living room carpet as one of his eyes slowly closed once more. Molly saw it. "It's no use winking at me either!" She inwardly smiled at his endearing ways.

After her coffee she got up and took her cup to the kitchen where she refilled his water bowl and measured out some more dog crunchies into his food bowl. Jack sniffed them half heartedly. He was tired from all the new things he'd seen that day and also the queasy feeling in his stomach hadn't gone away. Nevertheless he started to pick them up and carry them into the hall where he tried to bury and hide them. "I think you're a little hoarder," said Molly as she busied herself with house chores.

During the evening, Molly and Joe settled down to chat and watch the television once more. Jack sat on the floor watching them, feeling increasingly tired and queasy. Molly, noticing that he was quiet, checked him over, but came to the conclusion he was just tired after his busy day and so ordered an early bedtime, leaving Jack in the kitchen as she had the night before, with both his soft bed and a towel on the floor near to the door.

Left in the dark kitchen on his own, Jack scratched at the door and whimpered a little before ignoring his soft bed and settling down on the towel as he'd done the night before. He tried very hard to be brave and to go to sleep, but he started to get anxious and his fretful mind began to wander. He felt hot and a bit dizzy and his queasiness was becoming full nausea. His mouth started to water and soon he couldn't help himself and was violently sick all over the towel. He whimpered softly, but nobody heard him and so he lay shivering on the wooden floor beside his pool of vomit.

Upstairs, Molly was a little worried about Jack. She hadn't liked the way he had gone very quiet that evening, but told herself it was nothing, that he was just tired. She didn't hear the soft whimper from downstairs and so turned over and closed her eyes.

Jack was struggling. He lay dozing fitfully on the hard kitchen floor and his worries turned into nightmares. Enormous, dark cat claws scratched at his body, twisting into his gut and making him cry out in pain. Then he was falling, falling through water. Huge, sightless fish monsters bumped his body whilst he sucked in mouthfuls of dank, poisoned water. As he fell to the depths of the pond, a voice called to him, "Jack, Jack I'm here!"

He opened his eyes and saw a petite face of a Chihuahua, floating in front of him in the water. It was a face he remembered from his past. "Mum!" he gasped and drank in some more of the pond water. "Mum, is it really you?"

The face before him spoke, "Yes, I'm here! It's so good to see you once more." Jack's mother paused and then she said, "Jack, I'm bringing you a message from all the dogs that have gone before. Jack, you must fight, fight with all your might. Fight all the bad things that happen to you and find happiness."

Jack was struggling to breathe and forced himself to focus on her face. "Fight? Why bother? Look at what the humans did to you and how they treat us dogs. Why should I fight to stay?"

She was growing dimmer. "These new humans are your friends, they will treat you well. What happened to me, it wasn't intended. The human was just neglectful and didn't protect me from the Bigs. These humans are different, they will save you." She was fading now. "Fight Jack. Fight with all your strength."

The dark water was overwhelming and his mother was gone. The pain in his stomach from the cats' claws was excruciating and the fish monsters were stabbing his sides with their fins now. He was sinking and sinking into the darkness.

"Jack! Jack, wake up!" A voice was calling far above him. Tender fingers were lifting his broken body and holding him tight. He fought against the darkness and turned his head towards the voice. "That's it Jack, you're safe with me." He opened his eyes and he was lying in the arms of Molly who was sitting on the kitchen floor.

Molly hadn't been able to sleep for long. She'd woken up and worried about Jack, tossing and turning in bed. Finally, telling herself she was fretting over nothing, she decided she'd better get up and check that he was alright. She'd put on her slippers and dressing gown, trod quietly downstairs and opened the kitchen door.

What a sight met her eyes! Jack was lying on his side on the other side of the door, in a pool of vomit, the towel rucked up around him. His eyes were rolled back and his mouth was gaping open, gasping and crying whilst his paws were scrabbling on the hard kitchen floor. She bent down quickly, sitting beside him to pick up his weak body. As she called his name, he opened his eyes and slowly focused on her face. His movements slowed and his crying lessened. "Jack," she repeated, "it's alright, I'm here now." She held his shivering body close as he leant into her warmth.

They sat like that for several minutes, the tiny dog trembling in her arms as she stroked his fur and spoke his name. Finally, she judged him to be calmer and put him down on the floor for a moment whilst she straightened up. "Jack, I'm going to clean you up a bit and make you more comfortable." She spoke matter-of-factly but it hid her worry. *How had he got so ill, so quickly? What should she do?*

Her practical nature clicked in and she fetched various cleaning things and tidied up and mopped up the kitchen floor and popped the vomit stained towel into a bucket to soak. She cleaned up Jack once more, fortunately not much vomit had got into his fur so a damp sponge and a quick towel and he was much fresher. She thought she should let him relieve himself outside, so she accompanied him out into the garden where he was sick once again. Prepared this time, she quickly cleaned up and brought him back inside to warm up. Although it was a warm summer's night, Jack was shivering uncontrollably.

Molly made herself a cup of tea. She could see this was going to be a long night, and carried her drink into the living room where she put it down on a small table beside the settee. She then fetched a small fleece blanket and knelt down. "Now Jack, you be a good boy and I'll get you nice and warm." She picked up the tiny, quivering dog and sat down on the settee, wrapping him in the blanket and placing him on her knee as she did so. Jack lay quietly on her lap, looking up at her adoringly with his big brown eyes. *Mum was right, this human will look after me.*

Molly sat quietly and drank her tea and watched as Jack's eyes slowly closed and his breathing became more regular. He still had bouts of shivering, but these became fewer as time went on. Jack slept and Molly watched over him, all thoughts of her nice dog-free furniture banished as she silently prayed he would be alright. She sat up with him through the early hours of the morning as he fretfully changed position and she had to rewrap him in the fleece. Just before dawn, as her eyes were drooping, he seemed to fall into a deeper sleep and she allowed herself to doze.

"Mum! Mum, what's happened? Is Jack ill?" Jack awoke with a woof and Molly woke up with a start as she heard Joe call her name. She looked down and, noting Jack's improved condition, started to tell Joe the whole story.

A while later she concluded, "So you see, I think it was the pond water that made him ill. His little body hasn't had much exposure to outside dirt and so it overwhelmed him." She stroked Jack's head as he snoozed on her knee. "I think he can just have a quiet recovery day today, there'll be time for more outside adventures and walks when he's recovered. We'll need to keep his strength up, would you go and get me a couple of his dog crunchies?"

Joe nodded, but looked a little puzzled. "Mum, I thought you didn't want dogs on the furniture? How come you're going to feed him there now?"

Molly eyed him sheepishly. "I know, I know. But, you see, I just couldn't leave him on the hard floor, and you can see how much happier he is on my knee, he's settled right down. Get me some crunchies, would you?"

Joe could see her mind was made up and so he fetched the food and put it on the table next to Molly. For the next hour, Molly sat quietly with Jack on her knee, feeding him one crunchie at a time, slowly letting his stomach settle and his body recover.

Jack could feel his energy returning and the shivers subsiding. He lay there, gazing adoringly at Molly, taking the crunchies delicately from her fingers and eating them softly on her lap. His mother had been right, trust these humans, they would keep him safe. Especially this one, who gave him toys and fed him one crunchie at a time and stayed up with him all night. He stared up at Molly with his enormous brown child-like, Chihuahua eyes and thought one thing. *Mummy!*

Molly now realised for sure her life would never be the same again, with the care and the responsibility of this wee dog all on her shoulders. She welcomed the task, however. She knew the tiny dog needed careful nurturing and that she, in return, felt a strong need to nurture. Such was the chihuahua nature of him, delicate and needy. It had initially been masked by that Jack Russell coat of his, but he truly was a dog of both breeds. They sat together in harmony, both meeting a need in the other, dog child and human mother.

And so it was that Jack finally earned his full name, the one that would last him the rest of his life. Molly silently mouthed his name as she held and soothed him. *Jack Chi!*

The End

About the Author

May Conway was born and grew up in Cheshire. She was lucky enough to live in a pretty suburban home with parents who bred and rescued all sorts of small animals.

Now with grown children herself, and having moved away to the midlands, she continues the family traditions, having adopted and rehabilitated several rescue dogs.

Her stories, although fictional, are based on her observations of characters she has known. They bring to life the struggles, injustices and hopes faced by people and the animals they love.

Read more of her work at www.mayconway.wordpress.com

Printed in Great Britain
by Amazon